Wild Ivy

Hakuin
self-portrait

Wild Ivy

THE SPIRITUAL

AUTOBIOGRAPHY

OF ZEN MASTER

HAKUIN

Translated by
Norman Waddell

SHAMBHALA
Boston & London   2001

SHAMBHALA PUBLICATIONS, INC.
Horticultural Hall
300 Massachusetts Avenue
Boston, MA 02115
www.shambhala.com

Printed in the United States of America
⊗ This edition is printed on acid-free paper that meets
the American National Standards Institute z39.48 Standard.
Distributed in the United States by Random House, Inc.,
and in Canada by Random House of Canada Ltd

Library of Congress Cataloging-in-Publication Data
Hakuin, 1686–1769/
    [Itsumadegusa English]
    Wild ivy: the spiritual autobiography of Zen Master Hakuin
Itsumadegusa/translated by Norman Waddell.
      p. cm.
    ISBN 1-57062-435-6 (cloth)
    ISBN 1-57062-770-3 (paperback)
    1. Hakuin, 1686–1769.   2. Priests, Zen—Japan—Biography.
3. Spiritual biography—Japan.   I. Waddell, Norman.   II. Title.
BQ9397.E597H3513   1999
294.3'927'092—dc21   98-39907
[B]   CIP

BVG 01

CONTENTS

Translator's Introduction

Hakuin Ekaku (1686–1768) is a towering figure in Japanese Zen. Widely respected during his lifetime for the extraordinary courage and determination and uncompromising independence he displayed as he strove tirelessly to revive a Zen tradition in a state of deep spiritual stagnation and decline, during the two and half centuries since his death, he has assumed patriarchal significance in his school and has remained to this day an overshadowing presence whose life and work have become emblematic of the truths he espoused.

Part of the reason for the unique position Hakuin has continued to hold is undoubtedly to be found in the uncommon literary and artistic legacy he left behind. He excelled as a writer, painter, and calligrapher and used these talents fully over the final decades of his life as he tried to devise new ways of spreading the Zen teachings among people of all classes and walks of life. The result is a body of work—voluminous writings and countless ink drawings and calligraphic inscriptions—that is both a powerful expression of his prodigious, exuberant personality and a vivid testimony to his profound spiritual awakening.

Working within a tradition in which priests are unusually tight-lipped about their personal stories and autobiographies are almost nonexistent, Hakuin left a record of his life and religious experience that in both extent and detail is without parallel in Japanese Buddhism. This inclination to talk about his life increased with age, becoming in his seventies and eighties a prominent feature of his teaching style. It extended to his paintings as well. The well-known series of self-portraits he drew—themselves a form of autobiography—date from this period, as do his depictions of other Buddhist priests and familiar figures from Buddhist folklore, such as Bodhidharma and Pu-tai, many of whom bear an unmistakable resemblance to their creator. The persona Hakuin created of himself through his writings and visual art has for later generations of students epitomized the Zen life. In recent decades, it has gained him recognition beyond the confines of his native land as one of the world's truly great religious figures.

This book is a translation of Hakuin's spiritual autobiography *Wild Ivy* (Japanese, *Itsumadegusa*), which he wrote at the age of eighty-one, two years before his death. It is the longest and most comprehensive of the autobiographical narratives contained in his writings and the principal source for roughly the first three decades of his life—the period during which he was engaged in his struggle for enlightenment—containing many events and episodes that cannot be found elsewhere. As such, it has considerable value and interest as straight biography, both for the factual events it records of his life and for the vivid firsthand descriptions of the decisive episodes that occurred during this crucial period in his spiritual growth and development.

But Hakuin's principal motive for relating his story was clearly instructional. He believed that by telling others about his experiences, he could encourage them in their training and that in so doing he could clarify his basic approach to Zen study and help students avoid falling victim to contemporary teachings that he felt were destroying the Rinzai school's time-honored tradition of koan study. To this end, he frequently breaks the narrative to press home a point or lesson he believes to be of special importance to the student. These digressions—which tend to give *Wild Ivy* a somewhat episodic, disjointed quality—take the form of short moral tales, scathing attacks on the views of heretical contemporary Zen teachers, as well as direct exhortations of advice and caution to students.

Wild Ivy, like Hakuin's other autobiographical narratives, is related from the vantage point of the mature teacher. Events are shaped and reshaped through reflection and religious argument as well as by the dynamics of the storytelling itself. Certain themes and episodes that have come in the course of time to assume greater importance to him receive correspondingly more attention. The harm wrought by contemporary teachers with their doctrine of Unborn "silent illumination" Zen and the greatness of his teacher Shōju Rōjin are cases in point. As in any autobiography, there is some degree of exaggeration and embellishment, an occasional stretching and bending of the facts. Hakuin is usually the only source for the accounts he gives. Moreover, he relates many of his stories in more than one version. Inevitably, this gives rise to discrepancies and disparities of various kinds, which are at this point difficult, and sometimes impossible, to reconcile.

All that said, I believe the overall evidence still suggests that Hakuin's account of his life is accurate in its general outlines. Since my main purpose here is to translate what Hakuin wrote in *Wild Ivy*, I have limited myself in the supplementary notes to pointing out only such inconsistencies and contradictions as I felt to have some special interest.

HAKUIN'S LIFE

The following account of Hakuin's life is designed to provide a broader chronological background for the rather episodic narrative in *Wild Ivy*. In compiling it, I have tried to take into account all the primary sources. This means, for the first half of the life, relying almost exclusively on the personal recollections found in *Wild Ivy* and in *Goose Grass* (Japanese, *Yaemugura*), a work published in Japanese about ten years earlier that parallels much of the material in *Wild Ivy*; and for the second half, on Tōrei Enji's *Biography of Zen Priest Hakuin* (Japanese, *Hakuin Oshō Nempu*), which is virtually the only account we have for the fifty-year period of his teaching career. (Many of the short quotes about Hakuin in this introduction come from Tōrei's *Biography*.)

Hakuin Ekaku—to give him his full religious name—was born Nagasawa Iwajirō on the twenty-fifth day of the twelfth month of 1685 (January 19, 1686, by the Western calendar) in the small village of Hara, situated beneath the towering cone of Mount Fuji. Hara was a farming and fishing community, as well as a post station on the main Tōkaidō road, which linked the capital at Kyoto and the rapidly growing administrative center in Edo.

Moving toward the second century of Tokugawa rule, Japan was five years into the reign of Tsunayoshi, the notorious "Dog Shogun," and on the threshold of a period of unprecedented economic and cultural prosperity. The affair of the Forty-seven Rōnin, which stirred Tokugawa society perhaps more than any other single event, occurred a year before Hakuin set out on the first of a series of extended Zen pilgrimages that would occupy him on and off into his thirties. While he was engaged in his travels, eastern Japan was hit by several major natural disasters. In 1703, a severe earthquake, tidal waves, and fires caused much loss of life and great destruction in Edo and along the Tokaidō littoral. The last eruption of Mount Fuji, in 1707, devastated Hakuin's home province of Izu. Whole villages in the vicinity of Hara were swept completely away, buried under the tremendous onslaught of mud and rocky debris. Hakuin was home on a visit at the time.

While everyone else, including the incumbent of the temple where he was staying, fled to safety. Hakuin remained meditating inside the main hall of the temple, as countless sharp tremors rocked the buildings to their foundations.

Hakuin was the last of five children, three brothers and two sisters, born to the Nagasawa family, proprietors of the Omodaka-ya, an inn said to be of the *waki-honjin* class that was used as a stopover by chief lieutenants of the daimyo and in a pinch by daimyo themselves when they passed through Hara on their way to and from Edo.

Hakuin's father was born to a samurai family named Sugiyama. He assumed his wife's surname—Nagasawa—at the time of his marriage. Later, upon becoming head of the Nagasawa household, he also adopted the hereditary name Genzaemon and inherited the post of chief of the Hara station, whose duties included providing horses and porters for the daimyo processions, officials, merchants, and others who passed to and fro on the Great Eastern Road.

Hara may have been one of the smaller post stations on the Tōkaidō, but it was no sleepy backwater. Located along a heavily trafficked coastal stretch bordering Suruga Bay, it was by all accounts the scene of intense activity. The Dutch physician Engelbert Kaempfer, who passed through on his way to Edo in 1791 and again in 1793, described "Farra" as being a village of average size, consisting of about two hundred and fifty dwellings. Young Hakuin—he would have been eight at the time of Kaempfer's second visit—was most probably among the curious crowds of people who lined the road in front of the family inn to catch a glimpse of the passing entourage of outlandish-looking Dutchmen. In his book *Japanese Inn*, Oliver Statler gives a lively description of this area around Izu Province, portraying life at a similar *waki-honjin* inn, the Minaguchi-ya, at the Yui post station only three stops west of Hara. Hakuin himself, in one of his early writings, described the activity at the Mishima post station, three miles to the east:

> Mishima, long renowned as the jewel of Izu Province, is situated in a position of strategic importance unmatched in all the land, with the mountains of the Hakone Barrier soaring up before it and the Fuji River a fast-flowing boundary at its rear. Crowds of people throng the busy streets; among them are scoundrels drawn from all parts of the country. Gamblers and other miscreants who live their lives outside the law can be seen lurking in every corner . . . they ply their mischief with impunity in thousands of unsavory ways: forcing locks on warehouses, tunneling into the backs of go-downs, setting fires, then scattering through the neighboring counties, where they proceed to extort money from people or rob them outright. With all this going on around the Mishima post station, residents and visitors alike never experience a moment's peace day or night.[1]

Thanks to paintings and wood-block prints of the period, we are able to see how Hara and the surrounding countryside must have appeared in the eighteenth century. It was dominated by Mount Fuji, then as now awesome in its solitary grandeur. The prints depicting Hara in the various sets of Hiroshige's Tokaidō series show a huge, gray-white peak that fills the entire background, towering into blue sky above fields and foothills rising northward from the wayside village. Although neither the derivation nor the precise significance of the name *Hakuin*—which means literally "hidden white" or "hidden in whiteness"—is known, it is generally thought to be in some way connected to the great snow-covered peak that was a daily presence from his earliest years.

EARLY YEARS (1685–1699, BIRTH TO AGE 14)

The biographical accounts provide little information concerning the paternal side of Hakuin's family. The Sugiyamas were appar-

ently from a village named Nishiura not far from Hara. Tōrei
traces the family ancestry back to an illustrious warrior clan of the
Kamakura period whose leaders fought by the side of the celebrated Yoshitsune. One member of the family, a great-uncle of
Hakuin, was a Zen priest named Daizui. Daizui was reportedly
instrumental in arranging for the father's adoption into the Nagasawa family. He was also responsible for rebuilding the Shōin-ji,
a Zen temple in Hara where Hakuin's father is supposed to have
studied for a time during his youth. It was to Shōin-ji that Hakuin went, at the age of fifteen, to be ordained, and there he
returned in his early thirties to be installed as abbot. He would
reside and teach at this tiny country temple for the next fifty years
of his life, transforming it into a center of Buddhist practice
known throughout the country.

His mother's side of the family, the Nagasawas, were devout
Nichiren Buddhists. They hailed originally from the village of
Nagasawa at Minobu in the province of Kai, where Nichiren
Shōnin spent his last years and a spot sacred to members of the
Nichiren school. Hakuin seems to have been especially close to
his mother. He describes her as "a simple, good-natured woman
. . . who took pleasure in spontaneous acts of kindness and compassion." She took him with her to listen to sermons at the local
Nichiren temples, and it seems clear that her deeply religious nature had a profound influence on her young son. Although, upon
entering religious life, he turned to the Zen school, many of the
elements that distinguish his lifelong effort to reform Rinzai
Zen—his extraordinary energy and single-minded determination,
his vehement denunciations of those he deemed unorthodox—
seem somehow to have more in common with the militancy of
Nichiren's evangelistic zeal than they do with the teaching style
traditionally associated with the Zen school and may well be
traced at least in part to Hakuin's childhood environment.

The records of Hakuin's youth contain numerous episodes
that are included to illustrate an early, if not prenatal, disposition

to religious life. Though generally plausible, such stories are an indispensable element in conventional Japanese hagiography, and we have no way of knowing whether or when Hakuin is improving on the truth. In all the accounts, he emphasizes the abnormal fear that gripped him at the age of eleven, when he heard a famous Nichiren preacher describe in great detail the terrible punishments inflicted upon sinners who fell into one of the Eight Hot Hells. From that time on, he was tormented by the fear of having to face such a horrible retribution himself. It was this fear, he said, that drove him to seek a means of escaping such a fate. Deeply impressed by stories he had been told about Buddhist priests whose great virtue had enabled them to undergo harrowing ordeals that would be inconceivable to ordinary mortals, he embarked on a regimen of spiritual exercises himself—rising at first cockcrow, reciting sutras, dousing himself with buckets of cold water, performing prostrations, praying to the gods for their help. If we are to believe the *Biography*, these boyish attempts at religious practice continued for several years without producing any noticeable results. Attributing his lack of success to the distractions and defilements that were an unavoidable feature of life in the mundane world, he concluded that his only chance of escaping hell and its terrors lay in the priesthood—a pure and uncorrupted realm where he would be free to devote his time and attention exclusively to his religious concerns.

ORDINATION AND EARLY PILGRIMAGE
(1699–1708, AGES 14–23)

Hakuin's parents, who had at first opposed the notion of losing their young son to the priesthood, had by his fourteenth year finally come around to accepting the inevitable. They took him to Tanrei Soden, the elderly resident priest at the neighborhood

Shōin-ji, to receive the tonsure. Although Hakuin later portrayed Tanrei as "a broad-minded and especially capable priest," he also confesses rather sheepishly at one point in *Wild Ivy* that his teacher had actually belonged to "the tribe of do-nothing Zen teachers" whose pernicious influence on contemporary training he severely censured for undermining the true and time-honored traditions of the school.

In any event, for some reason—Tanrei's infirmity and advanced age are usually cited—Hakuin was sent almost immediately to the Daishō-ji, a sister temple in the neighboring town of Numazu. For the next three or four years, he served as an attendant to the resident priest Sokudō Fueki, performing the menial duties expected of a young novice and gaining a solid grounding in classical Chinese, the language of the Buddhist texts whose study would be an important part of his training.

One of the works he read while at Daishō-ji was the great *Lotus Sutra*—the most famous and popular of all the Mahayana sutras. The *Lotus* was also the central scripture of his mother's Nichiren school, so he must have already had some degree of familiarity with its content. Nevertheless, after reading it through from cover to cover, he reported being deeply disappointed to find "it consisted of nothing more than simple tales about cause and effect." He did not change this opinion of the *Lotus,* nor apparently even read it again, until the night of his final decisive enlightenment almost a quarter century later. He would then finally grasp its deep meaning and understand the reason why it was reputed to be the "king of sutras"—the greatest of the Buddha's preachings.

At eighteen, he left Daishō-ji for the Monks Hall at the Zensō-ji, a training temple located a short distance from Hara. He describes himself as setting out in high hopes, eager to start his formal training, his mind filled with the stories he had heard of the hardships illustrious Zen figures of the past had overcome in their struggle to reach enlightenment. These expectations were soon disappointed. At Zensō-ji, he found that the monks were not engaged in the long, grueling sessions of zazen he had anticipated. They were studying texts—at the time, a collection of Chinese Zen poetry. This was the first of many encounters he would have in the course of his subsequent travels with those he came to regard with great contempt as "purveyors of quietist do-nothing Zen."

A second blow, at the time perhaps more telling, soon followed. During his lectures, the head priest happened to comment on a verse that contained an allusion to the great Chinese Zen master Yen-t'ou. The head priest's remarks piqued Hakuin's interest in this master. He went to the temple library to find out more about Yen-t'ou's life and learned that he had been murdered by bandits; when they cut off his head, his death cry was heard for ten miles around. It was hard for young Hakuin to conceive: if such a great priest could not even protect himself from bandits in this world, what possible hope could an ordinary monk like himself have of avoiding the fiery torments of hell in the next? This discovery dashed all the hopes and aspirations Hakuin had invested in the Buddhist priesthood. Zen lost all interest for him. He came to regard it and all it represented with intense dislike: "The mere sight of a sutra or Buddhist image was now enough to turn his stomach."

One obvious course of action open to him—returning home and admitting his mistake—he rejected as being "too humiliating to even contemplate." Still, he had to make a decision about what to do with the rest of his life. Following a period of intense soul-searching, he convinced himself that inasmuch as he was powerless to influence his destiny in the next life, he might as well enjoy his present one while he could. Since scholarly pursuits had a natural appeal for him, he decided to immerse himself in the study of literature, painting, and calligraphy. Not only would it help divert him from the fears still gnawing at his mind; with hard work, he might even be able to earn his livelihood as an artist or a writer.

While at Zensō-ji, an incident occurred involving Hakuin and a young girl that affords us a rare glimpse of a less formidable, more human side of the master, one the religious biographies generally elect to pass over in silence. It seems that Hakuin was visiting the Ejiri post station near the temple to attend a perform-ance by a troupe of traveling players. They were reenacting the incident of the Forty-seven Rōnin, an event still very fresh in people's minds, having taken place only the year before, and a large audience had crowded in to watch. Midway through the performance the seating area, overburdened by the overflow crowd, suddenly collapsed, causing numerous injuries to those in the audience. When Hakuin saw the seats begin to give way, he immediately threw himself in front of a young girl who was standing next to him. His quick-witted action saved her from harm and earned him the lifelong gratitude of the girl's father, a wealthy kimono merchant. Hakuin became a regular visitor at the family home. The father was so taken with young Hakuin that he began to regard him as a prospective son-in-law. He even broached the idea of adopting him into the family. Hakuin, whose thoughts at this time were still firmly fixed on religious life, declined the offer.

In the spring of 1704, after a year's residence, Hakuin left the Zensō-ji. Traveling with twelve other young monks, he made his way west along the Tōkaidō to a temple named Zuiun-ji in the town of Ōgaki in Mino Province. He was attracted to the Zuiun-ji by reports that its abbot, a scholar-priest known as Baō Rōjin, "Old Man Baō," was a scholar of wide learning, with a temple that was said to have a particularly fine library. Baō turned out to be an extremely rough customer, with a particularly nasty temper, and the students who had arrived with Hakuin were soon discussing the need to move on and try their luck elsewhere. Hakuin, however, who seems to have respected Baō's ability more than he feared his bearishness, was determined not to be driven off. In the months that followed, he managed to develop a cordial, even affectionate, relationship with "the wild horse of Mino Province."

After studying Chinese and Japanese verse composition for several months at Baō's temple, Hakuin received word that his mother had died suddenly following a short illness. There is no mention of the event in *Wild Ivy*. In Tōrei's *Biography*, the reference is terse—"his grief was inconsolable"—but there can be little doubt the unexpected bereavement had a deeply sobering effect on young Hakuin and was, together with the deepening realization that scholarly pursuits did nothing to diminish mental anguish, responsible for the decision he reached in the course of the summer to return to his Zen pilgrimage.

Sometime during this same period, at the annual airing of the temple library, there took place one of the famous episodes in Japanese Zen history. The most elaborate version of the story is the one Hakuin relates in *Goose Grass*. It shows, among other things, that the fear of falling into hell was still eating at his mind:

> I had reached a total impasse . . . the fears still dominating my thoughts . . . no idea where to turn for help. Streams of tears ran unconsciously down my cheeks[;] . . . my gaze happened to go up to the veranda of the Guest Hall, where hundreds of books had been stacked on top of desks following the annual airing of the temple library. . . . I lit an offering of incense before the books, performed a score or so of prostrations, and prayed earnestly to the gods and Buddhas for their help . . . telling them how, four or five years after shaving my head, I was still at sixes and sevens, had no idea what to do with my life . . . which of the paths—Buddhism, Confucianism, or Taoism—I should follow. . . . I closed my eyes and slowly approached a pile of books on one of the desks. With

my thumb and forefinger, I reached out and fished blindly among
the stacks until I had fixed on a single volume. . . . I pulled it out
and raised it high above my head in veneration two or three times.
Then I opened it. . . .[2]

He had chosen a work titled *Spurring Students through the
Zen Barriers* (*Ch'an-kuan ts'e-chin*), a collection of anecdotes and
quotations relating to Zen study culled from a wide variety of Zen
and Buddhist texts. He opened the pages randomly, to a passage
describing the life and practice of the celebrated tenth-century
Chinese priest Tz'u-ming. While engaging in zazen through the
freezing nights of northern China, Tz'u-ming had jabbed himself
in the thigh with a needle-sharp awl whenever he sensed the
"sleep demon" approaching. To Hakuin, Tz'u-ming's serendipi-
tous intervention at this juncture could have only one meaning: a
person who commits himself to attaining religious awakening
must push forward with unwavering determination, whatever difficulties he encounters, until the goal is reached.

Tz'u-ming, it happens, was an extremely important figure in
Lin-chi Zen. He is credited with having kept the line alive when,
early in the Sung dynasty, it was on the verge of extinction. In
light of Hakuin's own self-imposed role as the reformer of a
moribund Japanese Zen, Tz'u-ming's appearance takes on an un-
canny, almost oracular, significance, one that can hardly have
been lost on Hakuin as he was composing his autobiographies.

Hakuin remained at Baō's temple until the following spring.
He then set forth on what would turn out to be an extended
pilgrimage that would occupy the next several years and take him
throughout most of central Japan and as far west as the city of
Matsuyama, on the island of Shikoku. The months he had spent
under Baō's tutelage developing his talents for poetry and calligraphy were by no means wasted. He would put them to good use
later during his teaching career, with great effectiveness, as he

began to take a more active interest in extending his Zen teaching beyond his immediate students to the populace at large.

Until this point, Hakuin had pursued his study more or less on his own, moving from temple to temple, seeking, without much success, to find a teacher in whom he could place his complete trust. His travels had, he says, given him a clear-eyed sense of what was wrong with contemporary Zen. Most of the teachers he encountered during this period—and they included noted masters of all three main Zen traditions—are described as being advocates of the passive, quietist religious practices he would later, in his writings, violently denounce for sapping students of the very thing—"a great burning tenacity of purpose"—he felt was absolutely essential to the religious quest. "Unless students press forward with a spirit of fierce and dauntless inquiry," he wrote, "they will never break free from Mara's net of delusion. It will cling to their bones, stick to their hides, until the last breath they draw."

As far as Hakuin was concerned, there was little need to distinguish between the "zazen-only" practices of contemporary Sōtō Zen, the Nembutsu Zen of the Ōbaku school, and the "do-nothing, Unborn" Zen espoused by most of the Rinzai priests he encountered. According to him, their plausible doctrines, working on the minds of impressionable young students, had badly undermined the true traditions of the school. The transgression could not have been more heinous, and accordingly, he turned all his power of sulfurous denunciation against them.

In the spring of his twenty-third year, Hakuin journeyed to the Eigan-ji in Takada, a flourishing city on the Japan Sea coast in Echigo Province. He gives two reasons for the visit: a lecture-meeting on a Zen text titled *The Eye of Men and Gods* (*Jen-t'ien yen-mu*) and reports of a senior Eigan-ji priest of such exceptional spiritual mettle that he had received Dharma sanction from masters of all three Zen schools. The first of these reasons seems to have been no more than a pretext, and his meeting with the senior priest left him unimpressed. It appears, in fact, that he spent almost the whole meeting off by himself practicing zazen. He had been wrestling steadily for some time now with the Mu koan, and signs had appeared over the past year of an approaching breakthrough. Wanting to be alone to focus on his zazen without distraction or interruption, he hid inside a shrine room he found at the back of the temple for a weeklong solitary retreat. As he was sitting there in the predawn hours on the final night, the sound of a distant bell reached his ears. As it did, he finally crossed the threshold into satori, or enlightenment. So intense was the experience, he was convinced that no one in the past three hundred years had penetrated to such a glorious attainment. He spent the next several weeks strutting around the temple, "puffed up with a soaring pride, bursting with arrogance . . . and swallowing whole everyone he encountered, regarding them contemptuously as so many lumps of dirt."

At this point, through another of those coincidences that almost seem designed to make Hakuin's life a paradigm for Zen training, he encountered the elderly priest Shōju Rōjin ("The Old Man of Shōju Hermitage"). It didn't take long for Shōju to deflate the young man's overweening pride and to disabuse him of the notion that his training was over.

SHŌJU RŌJIN (1708, AGE 23)

In Shōju, Hakuin seems to have found the teacher he had been seeking. In Hakuin's writings, Shōju comes across as something of a maverick. Living by choice in a tiny hermitage in an extremely isolated corner of the country, Shōju would have been totally outside the mainstream Zen world. He accepted few students and only those who convinced him they were totally dedicated and possessed the capacity to mature into genuine teachers themselves. To those students, Shōju was a fierce, uncompromising taskmaster whose methods were harsh in the extreme.

Hakuin was with Shōju for only eight months, but it is clear in reading his accounts of the period that they were the most important of his life. Hakuin said that until he met Shōju, he had believed it relatively easy to achieve religious attainment. Shōju's relentless hounding soon cleared his mind of that notion—"crushed it like an eggshell." Tōrei portrays Hakuin as being in a state of near terror the whole time he was with Shōju—"trembling in every joint, his flesh constantly puckered up in goosebumps." At one point, Shōju grabbed him and tossed him off the veranda onto the ground—"as if I were a little kitten," Hakuin later remembered. But Shōju assigned him a series of "hard-to-pass" koans, and in boring his way into them, he was successful in "dropping his bones and sinews" on three different occasions. These additional realizations deepened his understanding, gradually enabling him to appreciate why Shōju pressed him so vehemently to continue his practice; why when Shōju had asked his reason for becoming a monk, his reply—that he had done it because he was afraid of falling into hell—had brought the scornful retort: "You're a self-centered rascal, aren't you!" Not until eighteen years later, upon attainment of his final great enlightenment at the age of forty-one, would Hakuin fully grasp the significance of Shōju's reproach and with it the true meaning of "post-satori" practice. Years later, when Hakuin asked his student Tōrei this same question, Tōrei's answer—"To work for the salvation of my fellow beings"—brought a laugh from Hakuin. "A much better reason than mine," he said.

"Post-satori practice," which became a distinguishing feature of Hakuin Zen, can be said to have ended for Hakuin in the final great enlightenment mentioned above, which marked the completion of his monastic training. But in the larger sense in which Hakuin viewed it, post-satori practice was a continuing process; only the focus had changed. Now it was "the practice of teaching others." Often, in his writings, he equates this practice with Bodhichitta, the "Mind of Enlightenment," which he explains as "doing good by helping others and imparting the gift of the Dharma to them." Defined in this way, "post-satori training" is seen as the leitmotif and source of *Wild Ivy* and all his writings.

By winter, Hakuin says that he had succeeded in "penetrating the heart of Shōju's Zen." Shōju urged him to stay on as his successor at Shōju-an, but Hakuin refused the request and, in late autumn of 1708, returned to Shōin-ji. One factor in his decision to leave was the unexpected appearance at Shōju-an of the three monks who had accompanied him to Eigan-ji the previous year. They expressed their desire to stay on at the hermitage with Hakuin, who seems to have been the leader of the group. Knowing that their presence would prove disruptive, he had little choice but to leave Shōju-an with them.

Hakuin remained at Shōin-ji throughout the winter retreat, but when spring came, he was on the road once again. Over the next several years, he continued to travel widely, seeking out Zen teachers wherever he went to ask their advice about how he should proceed with his post-satori practice. Curiously, however, he never once during the remaining thirteen years of Shōju's life returned to the Shōju-an hermitage, nor is there evidence of any correspondence passing between the two men during that time.

Although there are a number of unanswered questions associated with Hakuin's relationship with Shōju Rōjin, the most difficult and most puzzling to account for—especially considering the way Hakuin lavishly praises Shōju's teaching ability and constantly professes his undying gratitude toward him—is this seeming neglect of his teacher. Iida Tōin, a highly regarded Zen master of the modern era, summarized the doubts felt by many readers of Hakuin's autobiographies when he wrote: "The master studied with Shōju for slightly more than eight months. Shōju lived for another thirteen years after that. Although it is true that Shōju's hermitage was located in a remote part of the country, it was not in some foreign land far across the sea. At the very least, Hakuin should have gone to spend the summer retreat each year with his teacher."

The most plausible explanation—to me, at least—is that Hakuin only realized the full extent of the debt he owed his teacher after Shōju's death. The following passage from the *Biography* would seem to support such a supposition:

> Whenever I heard Shōju deliver harsh judgments on other Zen teachers, I used to think to myself, "Why does the old fellow do that? Why does he get so riled up about respected temple priests, men known throughout the country for their great virtue?" I even wondered if the reason might not be because they belonged to a different teaching line. After I left him, though, I traveled the length and breadth of the land. I visited many different teachers, but not once during that time did I meet up with an authentic Zen master—not one person who possessed the true and absolute Dharma eye. I was then able to understand how far Shōju's Zen surpassed all the others.

Most of the accounts Hakuin gives of the decisive enlightenment that came to him unexpectedly in his forty-first year include the assertion that the experience enabled him to grasp for the first time the true nature of Shōju's Zen. Other indications in the writings also suggest that his realization of the indispensable role Shōju had played in his religious career occurred at this time. By his late fifties, when he began to devote himself in earnest to his literary activity, he is extolling Shōju as the only authentic Zen teacher of the age and acknowledging him unequivocally as his one and only master.

POST-SATORI PRACTICE
(1709–1716, AGES 24–31)

During the travels that followed his return to Shōin-ji, it became clear to Hakuin that his attainment was still incomplete. He had no doubts about the depth of his enlightenment, he was sure that his grasp of koans and Zen writings was sharp and clear, yet he found it impossible to sustain the tranquillity he experienced in the quietness of the Zen hall when he returned to the tumult of everyday life.

"I feel like a physician who possesses a wonderful knowledge of medicine but has no effective means of curing an actual sickness," he lamented. "How can I possibly hope to help rid other sentient beings of their afflictions as long as I still suffer from illness myself?" With renewed determination, he now "grasped the whip in hand and spurred the dead ox forward once again." The focus of his post-satori training was directed henceforth to achieving the total integration of the two aspects of his life, the quiet and the active.

He was in the provinces north of Edo in the winter of 1711, his twenty-sixth year, when word reached him that his teacher Sokudō was terminally ill and had no one to care for him. He immediately returned to the Daishō-ji to nurse his old teacher.[3] He stayed into the following year, preparing Sokudō's food and medicine but devoting all his free time to zazen—"never sitting for less than eight sticks of incense each night"—and to reading widely in Zen and Buddhist literature—"illuminating his mind with the teachings of the ancients." Hakuin stayed until summer, when an unexpected offer of help from a fellow monk allowed him to return to the Shōin-ji. It was there in late summer he received the news that Sokudō had passed away.

Hakuin now set out once again on his travels. This time, they took him back to western Japan—Ise and Wakasa Provinces and the areas around Kyoto and Osaka. Among the temples he visited was the Hōun-ji, an Ōbaku temple in Kawachi Province, where he went to seek the advice of the eighty-one-year-old master Egoku Dōmyō. Although the account of his interview with Egoku in *Wild Ivy* has Hakuin asking Egoku how to deal with his "Zen sickness," according to the *Biography*, he sought help in overcoming the lack of freedom he still felt when he pursued his practice amid the busy come and go of daily life. Although it is difficult to say with certainty which of these accounts is correct, Egoku's suggested course of action—"Go and live in the mountains and be prepared to remain there, withering away with the trees and plants, until you find your way through"—would seem more appropriate as a remedy for Zen sickness.

For the next year or so, acting on Egoku's advice, Hakuin wandered from place to place, searching without success for a hermitage where he could isolate himself for a solitary retreat. One of the first places he visited was the Inryō-ji, a Sōtō temple in Izumi Province. There the abbot and senior priests were reportedly so impressed by Hakuin that they asked him to stay on and become the resident priest. Hakuin seems to have given the offer serious consideration. But he had difficulty arriving at a decision, and finally, with the matter still unresolved, he set out for other parts.

Although the practice methods of contemporary Sōtō teachers come in for a good deal of extremely hostile comment later in Hakuin's writings, during his travels, he seems to have visited many Sōtō temples. Dōgen, the founder of the school, is frequently quoted and always mentioned in terms of the greatest respect. Had Hakuin accepted the offer from the Inryō-ji, it is intriguing to reflect how a person with his extraordinary energy and talents might have influenced the course of later Sōtō Zen.

In spring of 1715—at the age of thirty—well over a year after the start of his search, Hakuin finally succeeded in locating a remote spot deep in the mountains of Mino Province suitable for a solitary retreat. There, living by himself in a tiny hut completely isolated from the world, subsisting on a ration of half a handful of rice each day, he began to carry out the instructions Egoku had given him to "wither away with the trees and plants."

ZEN SICKNESS

As I have already mentioned, at some point between his departure from Shōju and the time he returned to reside in the Shōin-ji— that is, between his twenty-fourth and thirty-first years—Hakuin contracted an ailment that he calls "Zen sickness" or "meditation sickness" (*Zenbyō*). Although the exact nature of the disorder is not known, from the description he gives of its symptoms, modern writers have diagnosed it variously as tuberculosis, pleurisy, nervous collapse, or some combination of the three. Whatever it was, it finally became so serious that it prevented him from pursuing his Zen training. The story of his struggle against Zen sickness and the cure he achieved by practicing techniques of meditation he learned from the hermit Hakuyū are the subject of the work known as *Idle Talk on a Night Boat* (Japanese, *Yasenkanna*). Since Hakuin uses the text of this work almost verbatim as the fourth chapter of *Wild Ivy,* I shall reserve any additional comment about Hakuyū and the visit Hakuin is supposed to have made to him for the supplementary notes to Chapter 4. What concerns us here are the conflicting dates Hakuin gives for his illness, which range from his twenty-fifth year, just after he left Shōju, all the way up into his early thirties, prior to the time he returned to reside at Shōin-ji. Although, under the circumstances, no definitive dating of the illness is possible, I believe the chronology proposed by Katō Shōshun, a modern authority on Hakuin's life, is a plausible one. Katō suggests Hakuin's late twenties as the most likely period, placing the onset of the sickness during the several years prior to the solitary retreat at Mount Iwataki. He also conjectures that the techniques of meditation described in *Idle Talk on a Night Boat,* which Hakuin says cured him, were probably those he had worked out on his own, a combination of traditional medical and meditation texts and folk therapies current at the time.

In any event, Hakuin lived at the hut on Mount Iwataki for well over a year, pushing himself mercilessly, fasting and going without sleep for days at a time, determined not to let up in his efforts until he achieved a further breakthrough, even if it cost him his life. He would have continued indefinitely what he calls the pleasures of this austere existence had it not been for the unexpected arrival of a family servant named Yake Shichibei. Shichibei had come to bring him the news that his father was dangerously ill and eager for him to return home and reside in the Shōin-ji, which was now without a priest. Hakuin, unable to ignore the urgent pleas of the faithful old servant, agreed to go back. He did so, he later said, with every intention of returning to his mountain hermitage at the first available opportunity. In fact, his decision to return marked the end of his long years of Zen pilgrimage.

SHŌIN-JI/GREAT ENLIGHTENMENT
(1716–1726, AGES 31–41)

Hakuin found the Shōin-ji totally impoverished and in an almost indescribable state of disrepair. The previous resident, Tōrin Soshō, an elder brother in the Dharma to Hakuin, seems to have fled the temple under a cloud. While chronic ill health and profligate habits (unspecified) are cited as reasons for his departure, the impossible living conditions no doubt also played a part.

"At night, stars shone through the roofs. Floors were sodden with rain and dew. . . . The halls had no doors or panels. Temple assets had passed into the hands of creditors, and the equipment for ceremonies and other temple furnishings had all been pawned. . . . About the only assets worthy of notice were the moonlight and the sound of the wind."

Thirteen months after his return, Hakuin was officially installed as head priest at Shōin-ji. The same year, 1718, he received from the Myōshin-ji headquarters temple the title of *Dai-ichiza*, or First Monk. It was the minimum rank required by government regulation for those installed as temple priests and seems to have been little more than a matter of paying a fee and registering Hakuin as the incumbent at Shōin-ji. It was apparently at this same time that he was given (or probably adopted on his own) the religious name—Hakuin—by which he has come to be best known.

Hakuin resided at this ramshackle old temple, amid great difficulty and privation, through his thirties and on into his early forties. An old family servant gathered wood for fuel, foraged for vegetables, and managed to produce the two daily meals. A monk who showed up helped supply the kitchen by making daily begging expeditions. Provisions were always meager, and the temple cook was usually forced to use spoiled or maggot-ridden food that had been rescued from the garbage the villagers were about to throw out.

During the first ten years at Shōin-ji, Hakuin attracted little attention outside his home province of Suruga. He seems to have remained at the temple, his time taken up with private retreats, with occasional lectures to the small number of monks and laypeople who came to him for instruction, and with running the temple affairs. Several anecdotes in the *Biography* give us an idea of the rigors of Hakuin's spare, simple life at the Shōin-ji during this period. When the sun went down, he would climb inside a derelict old palanquin and seat himself on a cushion he had placed on the floorboard. One of the young boys studying at temple would come, wrap his body in a futon, and cinch him tightly into this position with a rope. There he would remain, "like a painting of Bodhidharma," until the boy came and untied him the following day. A special room was built behind his living quarters where he could go and devote himself quietly to zazen. Neither did he neglect his study of Zen writings and other Buddhist texts: "The words and sayings of the Buddhas and Zen patriarchs never left his side. He used them to illuminate the old teachings by means of the mind, to illuminate the mind by means of the old teachings."

The religious quest that had been the single focus of his life for more than a quarter century finally came to an end one night in his forty-first year. He was in his chambers at Shōin-ji reading the *Lotus Sutra*, the very same chapter, the one on parables, he had dismissed years before as "a mere collection of simple tales about cause and effect." In that chapter, the Buddha reveals to his disciple Shariputra the true nature of the Mahayana Bodhisattva, whose own enlightenment is but the first step in his career of assisting others to attain theirs. This is identical to the teaching Shōju had tried to drive home to Hakuin years before. Like Shariputra, Hakuin had erroneously regarded his original realization as full and perfect enlightenment, and he would have been unable to proceed beyond that realization without the timely assistance of a genuine teacher.

As Hakuin read, the sound of a cricket churring at the foundation stones of the temple reached his ears; at that instant, he crossed the threshold into great enlightenment. The accumulated doubts and uncertainties of forty years suddenly ceased to exist. The reason why the *Lotus Sutra* was regarded as supreme among all the Buddha's preachings was revealed to him "with blinding clarity." He found teardrops "cascading down his face like strings of beads—they poured out like beans from a ruptured sack." From that time forth, wrote Tōrei, "the master lived in a state of great emancipation. The enlightening activity of the Buddhas was now his, without any lack whatever, enabling him to speak with the same tongue, and from the same lips, as all the Buddhas before him."

Over the remaining forty-two years of his life, Hakuin would exercise to the hilt this newly acquired ability to express his religious experience, as he now turned the focus of his formidable energies to teaching others. Books such as *Spurring Students through the Zen Barriers* and *The Three Teachings of the Buddha-Patriarchs* had played a decisive role in his own monastic development, and this must have convinced him of the important role writing could play in helping to spread his Zen teaching. He sometimes referred to the practice of writing as "the exercise of verbal *prajna*," which he further described as "a word or two from an enlightened teacher designed to trouble later generations of students."

TEACHING OTHERS (1726–1768, AGES 41–83)

The only extensive account of the teaching that occupied the second half of Hakuin's life is found in Tōrei's *Biography*. Reading it, one can only be amazed at the single-minded devotion and tireless energy he gave to the task. His entire life, right up until the year of his death, was centered in his effort to reform and reinvigorate the Zen school. He was constantly encouraging students to strive for the same profound penetration he had attained and devising new ways to reach out to the general populace and make them aware of the benefits of koan Zen. The *Biography* gives a fairly complete record of the scores of journeys he made around the country, some of many days' duration, in answer to endless requests for teaching and lectures; the writings he published, many first issued at his own expense in temple printings sponsored by Shōin-ji; and stories of encounters and confrontations he had with students and other priests.

In 1732, six years after the great enlightenment, more than twenty monks were residing and studying at Shōin-ji. Over the next few years, Hakuin lectured at the Shōin-ji on a number of important Zen texts, among them the famous *Blue Cliff Record*. In 1737, at the age of fifty-two, he conducted his first lecture-meeting at the request of another temple: a four-day session on the *Blue Cliff Record* at the nearby Rinzai-ji in Izu Province, which was attended by more than two hundred people. Similar invitations began coming in, obliging him to spend an increasing amount of his time on the road. This phase of his teaching activity culminated in a large-scale lecture assembly on the *Record of Hsi-keng*, which was held at the Shōin-ji in his fifty-fifth year. More than four hundred students took part. Hakuin availed himself of the opportunity to deliver a full-blown treatise on Zen, incorporating virtually all his basic views on teaching and training. It was his way of announcing himself to the world and proclaiming his determination to reform the school by purging it of the false doctrines and erroneous approaches to practice he believed were directly responsible for the precarious state of contemporary Zen. The meeting marked a major turning point. "From that time on," said Tōrei, "the master was recognized as the foremost teacher in the land."

One of Hakuin's students is said to have remarked that "if that old teacher of ours were lecturing from the high seat at a great and important temple, the whole world would be beating a path to his door." But—and this is a measure of Hakuin's greatness—people started doing that anyway. Seasoned monks began filing in from all parts of the country. As there was no way the Shōin-ji could house or provide for such large numbers, the monks were obliged to fend pretty much for themselves. They found lodgings as best they could in the countryside around the temple. Spread over a radius of three or four leagues, they transformed the surrounding woods and hills into a great center of Buddhist practice. Hakuin advised them to form into groups of three. They were to go out and find deserted halls, shrine buildings, or vacant houses that weren't being used and shut themselves up inside. There they would be able to devote themselves to undisturbed sessions of zazen.

It was unprecedented. A religious center that had risen up spontaneously, created by the students themselves, who had come for purely religious motives, drawn there in hopes of receiving instruction from Master Hakuin. A well-known passage from *Idle Talk on a Night Boat* gives some idea of the difficulties they faced:

> Students gladly endured the poisonous slobber the master spewed at them. They welcomed the stinging blows from his stick. The thought of leaving never even entered their minds. Some stayed for ten, even twenty years, totally indifferent to the possibility they might have to lay down their lives at Shōin-ji and become dust under the temple pines. . . . Hunger awaited them in the morning. Freezing cold lurked for them at night. They sustained themselves on greens and wheat chaff. Their ears were assaulted by the master's deafening shouts and abuse. Their bones were hammered by furious blows from his fists and stick. What they saw furrowed their foreheads in disbelief. What they heard bathed their bodies in cold sweat. . . . When they first arrived at Shōin-ji, they possessed the beauty of a Sung Yü or Ho Yen, their complexions glowing with radiant health. But before long, they were as thin and haggard as a Tu Fu or Chia Tao, their pallid skin drawn taut over their bony cheeks. . . . Would a single one of these monks have remained at Shōin-ji even a moment if he had not been totally dedicated to his quest, grudging neither his health nor life itself?

Until his mid-sixties, Hakuin's main teaching activity continued to focus on these full-time Zen students, both at the Shōin-ji and at other temples in the neighboring provinces where he was invited to teach. In the winter of 1750—at the age of sixty-five—he undertook a much longer journey, traveling all the way to Harima Province, west of Osaka, to deliver a series of lectures at the Ryōkoku-ji. The following spring, he moved to teach at several temples in neighboring Bizen Province. He stopped over in Kyoto on his way home, remaining there for several months, teaching at the residence of a wealthy layman named Yotsugi Masayuki. Among the lay students who came to receive instruction from him while he was in Kyoto was the great *bunjin* painter Ike Taiga.

It was during this same general period that Hakuin began to give more attention to his writing activity. His first publication— *Talks Introductory to Lectures on the Record of Hsi-keng* (*Sokkō-roku kaien-fusetsu*)—appeared in 1743, his fifty-eighth year. This was followed in 1746 by *A Record of Sendai's Comments on the Cold Mountain Poems* (*Kanzan-shi Sendai-kimon*) and four years after that by *Dream Words from the Land of Dreams* (*Kaian-kokugo*). These three works, among the most important of his writings, are records of his discourses and Zen lectures and were intended primarily for advanced students, those well versed in the difficulties of traditional Chinese Zen literature. They show the mature Hakuin at the height of his powers, a fearsome, uncompromising Zen master, whose "lightning thrusts" were described by students as having "a sharpness and force that made it impossible to even approach him."

He was, at the same time, taking his first concerted steps to spread his message among another constituency, and to the villagers of Hara and the general populace in the surrounding countryside, Hakuin was anything but unapproachable. He was apparently utterly determined that all people should share in the benefits of his Zen teaching. Distinctions of rank, class, or gender were almost meaningless when set against the all-important matter of kenshō—spiritual self-awakening achieved by seeing into the true nature. "In this universe, there is a great treasure," he once told people. "If you possess it, then whether you are a boatman or a cartman, a servant or a maid, you are a person of great fortune and virtue and wisdom. If you don't possess it, then even if you are an emperor, a daimyo, with high rank and great wealth, you are poor and ignorant, a person of low estate."

Up until the year of his death, an increasing share of Haku-in's time and effort was devoted to the needs of this new and expanding audience. The common touch that informs his teaching at this grassroots level is exemplified by the simple ink drawings he produced by the thousands for the endless stream of peasants and villagers who came to request them. For them as well, over the last fifteen years of his life, he composed dozens of written works, both prose and verse, in a baffling variety of styles and genres. Some were composed in ordinary Japanese vernacular, but others, borrowing from the popular culture of the time, were cast in the vulgar language and rhythms of country dialect. Crazy poems, nonsense verse, folk tales, parodies of popular songs, street doggerel, spiels for patent medicines, even riddles—they all became vehicles to convey his teaching of kenshō. And it is a tribute to his uncommon literary talent that he was able to carry this off without really diluting that teaching.

This same inventiveness and desire to find better ways of bringing people to the central experience of kenshō led him to devise a number of new and original koans, including the famous Hear the Sound of One Hand—which, from his mid-sixties on, he began assigning to beginning students in place of the traditional Mu koan.

When I was twenty-one or twenty-two, I kindled a great resolve and applied myself day and night with intense and single-minded devotion to the Mu koan. One night in . . . my twenty-third year, . . . I experienced a sudden great awakening. Wanting somehow to make it possible for others to acquire the power . . . to penetrate the Great Matter as well, I have guided and taught them from that time until this very day, over forty-five years. Not just my relatives and friends, but all people, including the old and young and those of high and low estate. I have had them raise doubts about their Self, I have given them the Mu koan to work on, I have used a variety of expedient means; . . . there must have been well over a score of them who were able to experience the tremendous joy of achieving awakening.

Then, about five or six years ago, I hit upon the idea of instructing my students by telling them all to hear the sound of the single hand. I have found it to be an infinitely better way of instructing people than the methods I had used before. Students who use it have a much easier time raising the mass of doubt, and they make much greater progress as they work on it during zazen. Its superiority to the former methods is like the difference between cloud and mud.[4]

Hakuin seems for most of his career to have steered clear of the great monastery complexes of Kyoto, not only during his period of pilgrimage but also later as a teacher when he lectured at temples in provinces around the capital. As for the Myōshin-ji headquarters temple with which Shōin-ji was affiliated, there is evidence that at least some of the ranking clerics were aware of the activities of this maverick country priest in the eastern provinces. One of these men, the eminent scholar-priest Muchaku Dōchū, made a special note in his diary of a pair of large scrolls of Hakuin's calligraphy that were hanging in the place of honor in one of the Myōshin-ji's main chambers. Judging from the date of the diary entry, they would be relatively early examples, probably from Hakuin's late fifties, before his calligraphy had acquired the simple yet monumental force of his later style, yet Dōchū still marveled over the "inexpressible strength and vitality" of the brushwork.

In his sixty-sixth year, during a three-month sojourn in Kyoto, Hakuin was invited to deliver lectures at the Myōshin-ji and at the equally large and important Tōfuku-ji. He took as his text the *Blue Cliff Record*. Among those who took part in the Myōshin-ji meetings were the abbesses of three imperial temples, one of them a daughter of the emperor.

Remarks that Hakuin made at a lecture-meeting in his seventy-fourth year clearly show the confidence he now felt in the depth and maturity of his understanding: "Whatever I hold up to elucidate for you—even if it is only a shard or a pebble—is transformed into a piece of purest gold. Where I am now, even when I'm sitting and joking and chatting informally with people, I'm turning the great Dharma wheel."

Four years later, in the spring of 1763, a general debility brought on by illness and old age became increasingly evident. Hakuin's students could see that the master's former vitality and alertness were no longer there. Lecturing left him exhausted. "It was as though the immense energy he had been pouring into his teaching activity were now used up." By midwinter, the decline was even more pronounced. The monks had planned a final lecture-meeting for the master the following spring. They now feared he might be unable to take part. While Hakuin showed little inclination to cut back on his teaching duties, he nonetheless felt compelled more and more to "share the lecture seat" with his disciple Tōrei and others. The following year, he officially retired as abbot of Shōin-ji, turning the position over to his student Suiō Genro.

In the spring of his eighty-first year, after hanging out a notice announcing he would no longer accept students for instruction, Hakuin traveled by palanquin to Edo for an extended stay at his student Tōrei's newly completed temple. For the six months he was there, he is said to have taught every day, his students including a number of high-ranking government officials.

Hakuin spent most of the following spring and summer relaxing and enjoying the waters at a hot spring on the Izu Peninsula, but winter found him at the Ryūtaku-ji, a temple he had recently constructed in neighboring Mishima, lecturing on his Zen records, *Poison Stamens in a Thicket of Thorns* (*Keisō Dokuzui*). The assembly was attended by more than two hundred and fifty monks—many of them former students—who had converged on the Ryūtaku-ji from all parts of the country for what they no doubt felt would be their farewell to the master. Partway through the lectures, he became too weak to continue and was obliged to turn the lecturing over to Tōrei.

He saw in the New Year (1768) at the Ryūtaku-ji. At the close of the winter training session, he was forced to take to his sickbed with an ailment that his physician diagnosed as "too many sugared sweets" and that may have been an attack of diabetes. A purgative was prescribed, which, in conjunction with some unstinting sleep, enabled him to recover his strength. He felt healthy enough later in the year to respond to requests for lectures from three nearby temples. At two of them, he gave several days of talks "on whatever moved his fancy." Again, the exertion exhausted him, but when one of his monks tried to suggest he should stop teaching, at least until he felt a little stronger, the reply was typical: "What's my fatigue, compared with the great hunger my students suffer?"

The account of Hakuin's final months is perhaps best taken directly from Tōrei's *Biography:*

> In the eleventh month, the master returned to Shōin-ji. It was clear his condition was growing more serious.
>
> On the sixth of the twelfth month, a freak storm swept the area, sending bolts of lightning crashing violently to earth. The next day, the physician Furugōri came to examine the master's pulses.

"What do you think?" the master asked.

"Nothing out of the ordinary," he replied.

"Can someone be called a skilled physician when he can't even tell when a patient has only three more days to live?" the master chided.

Old Mr. Yamanashi was allowed to visit. A go board was brought out, but after two or three moves, the master was forced to stop.

On the tenth day, the master called his disciple Suiō to his sickbed and entrusted him with his personal affairs after his death.

At daybreak the following day, the master was sleeping very peacefully, lying on his right side. He made a single loud groan, "UNNN," and then passed away.

The funeral was held on the fifteenth. A violent storm of wind and rain forced the cremation to be postponed until the following day. Afterwards, a great many relics were found among the ashes. . . . They resembled precious blue gems—the true fruits of the master's life of meditation and wisdom. Crowds of people flocked to the cremation site, more than a few of them comporting themselves like the demons who thronged to the Buddha's cremation hoping to acquire relics from his remains. Because of this, the relics were divided into three lots and enshrined in stupas at the master's three temples.

Two years after his death, Hakuin was awarded by imperial order the honorific *Zenshi*, or "Zen master," title *Shinki Dokumyō*. In 1884, the Emperor Meiji awarded him the *Kokushi*, or "National Master," title *Shōshū*, the final Kokushi title to be conferred in Japan.

WHAT WAS HAKUIN LIKE?

Tōrei described Hakuin as having "the heavy, deliberate motions of an ox and the penetrating glare of a ferocious tiger." This portrayal is confirmed by the life-size effigy statue of the master, which even today stares intimidatingly back at the viewer from its place of enshrinement in the Founder's Hall at the Shōin-ji, by the numerous self-portraits, and by the accounts of his students. He was a large, imposing figure of a man, in whom were combined great physical strength and a dominating character distinguished by extraordinary determination and uncompromising independence.

He was of course not all strictness and severity, however. Glimpses of a less daunting, more human Hakuin can be seen in some of the supplementary notes Tōrei added to his *Biography*, which contain anecdotes about his teacher's habits and foibles that enable us to gain a fuller picture of his overall personality.

He was, for example, inordinately fond of sweets. This weakness must have been well known in Zen circles, for Tōrei said that when he arrived at Shōin-ji for his first meeting with the master, he took as a gift a bag of sugared goodies he had picked up along the way. Hakuin was also extremely fond of soba noodles, and when the temple cook began preparing *tororojiru*, a dish made from pulverized mountain yam, we are told "the mere sound of the pestle grinding the yam was enough to make the master's mouth water and his eyes narrow with anticipation." Also, like most Japanese priests, he enjoyed drinking sake. The *Biography* tells of an incident in his mid-twenties when he stopped off to have a few last cups of sake before entering a temple to begin a rigorous practice session. According to the Zen historian Rikugawa Taiun, Hakuin allowed no sake in the Shōin-ji during his first ten years as head priest; later on, however, he drank moderately, saying it was for "medicinal purposes" only. He also had a pipe habit, dating back at least to his mid-twenties. At one point, troubled by the notion that his smoking might violate the Buddhist precepts, he decided to swear off. Taking out his tobacco pouch and *kiseru* pipe, he threw them into a rice paddy and then, as if to sever all remaining ties to the articles, poked them down with his staff until they were deeply buried in the mud. Again, he resumed the habit later on in life, this time saying it helped him to "relax from the demands of his teaching duties." Tōrei, a priest who was known for his strict adherence to the precepts, writes how he would sometimes enter Hakuin's chambers and catch the master hastily concealing his still smoking pipe behind his back.

THE TEXT

The original text of *Wild Ivy* consists of four parts: three *kan*, or fascicles, the second of which is in two sections. For convenience, I have converted these divisions into four numbered chapters; headings have for similar reasons been inserted throughout the text.

The title Hakuin chose for his work, *Itsumadegusa*, is the popular name for two common plants: the *kizuta* (*hedera rhombea*), or wild ivy, and the *mannengusa* (*sedum lineare*). We don't know which of these weeds Hakuin had in mind, but his title seems to suggest characteristics of both plants. The word *itsumade-gusa*—literally, "until-when grasses" or "how-long grasses" (the three Chinese characters for "wall," "growing," and "grass"), which in earlier Japanese literature commonly symbolized the brevity of worldly existence—may at the same time be descriptive of the plant's tendency to climb and proliferate indefinitely and perhaps thus contains a humorous poke at Hakuin's undeniable penchant for long-windedness.

In *Wild Ivy*, Hakuin mentions a god whom he calls Itsumadegusa myōjin, or Wild Ivy deity. He declares that as long as this deity stands guard, the Zen Dharma will never disappear entirely, even when the "winds of false teachings sweep the land." The name *Itsumadegusa myōjin* was apparently invented by Hakuin and may indicate the role he expected his written teaching to play, even after his death, in keeping later generations of students on the right path. The word *mannengusa*—literally, "ten thousand year" (or perennial) grass—would, of course, have similar connotations.

Wild Ivy is written in a peculiar style of Chinese *kanshi* verse that is apparently influenced by a humorous verse form known as *kyōshi*, or "mad poetry," which was fashionable during the second half of the eighteenth century and which reached the height of its considerable popularity at about the time Hakuin was writing.

The verses are composed in a basic seven-character line, and at first glance, it appears they can be read according to the conventions traditionally used for construing Japanese *kanshi* poetry—that is, by rearranging the words to conform with classical Japanese syntax. What sets Hakuin's Chinese verses apart is that they usually do not yield their meaning unless they are read as if they were composed in a highly vernacular—sometimes vulgar—Japanese idiom, laced with the puns and other verbal eccentricities typical of the "mad poetry" genre.

Although this may not have created much of a problem for Hakuin's contemporaries, it presents an almost insurmountable barrier for most modern readers of the work and no doubt accounts for the fact that *Wild Ivy* remains largely unknown to the Japanese themselves—unfortunately, for it is, after all, the personal record, extremely rare in Zen and Buddhism as a whole, of one of their greatest religious figures.

Hakuin's reasons for adopting such a bizarre medium for his autobiography are unclear. It may be he was counting on the current vogue for this verse form to attract a wider readership. It is also possible that it was just a way he had found of enjoying his final years. No doubt the answer lies in a combination of these explanations. Whatever the case, it is generally difficult to give in translation any idea of the intrinsic interest to be found in a kind of verse that depends for its effects largely on verbal wit and ingenuity and is, it must be admitted, poetry in form alone. Following several modern Japanese editions, which convert the Chinese verse into a more accessible form of simplified literary Japanese, I have translated it entirely as prose.

The appendix contains a translation of the preface to the famous work *Yasenkanna* (*Idle Talk on a Night Boat*), which had been published as an independent book, with the preface attached, about ten years before *Wild Ivy* was written. When Hakuin decided to include the text of *Yasenkanna* almost verbatim as Chapter 4 of *Wild Ivy*, he was, of course, obliged to omit the preface. I have included it in the appendix if for no other reason than that it contains a detailed description of an important technique of Introspective Meditation (*Naikan*) that is alluded to in Chapter 3 of *Wild Ivy*.

Dates are given as they appear in the text—according to the lunar calendar in use in pre-Meiji Japan and not converted to the Western calendar. This means, for example, that, according to Western calculation, Hakuin's birth (the twenty-fifth day of the twelfth month of 1685, lunar calendar) and death (the eleventh day of the twelfth month of 1768, lunar calendar) would both fall in the following year, January 19, 1686, and January 18, 1769, respectively. I have, however, altered the Japanese system of calculating age, which counts a person one year old at birth, to the extent of deducting one year from the ages given in the original text.

Wild Ivy was published in 1766. Some editions dated that year bear the imprint of Hakuin's temple Shōin-ji; others that of the Shidō-an, the temple in Edo where Hakuin's disciple Tōrei Enji was residing. The present translation is based on the Shidō-an wood-block edition as well as the *yomikudashi* version of that text found in Tokiwa Daijō's *Hakuin Zenji Shū*. For the last chapter of *Wild Ivy*, which contains a version of Hakuin's popular *Idle Talk on a Night Boat* that differs somewhat from earlier recensions of that text, I have also used *Yasenkanna furoku*, an edition of *Idle Talk on a Night Boat* recently issued by the Institute for the Study of Zen Culture of Kyoto.

I would like to acknowledge a special debt to two works: *Hakuin Oshō Shōden* (*A Detailed Biography of Priest Hakuin*), by Rikugawa Taiun, and *Hakuin Oshō Nempu* (*A Chronological Biography of Priest Hakuin*), by Katō Shōshun. The former has been a valuable source of information on many aspects of Hakuin's life and teaching; the annotations and index to the latter work have been very helpful in identifying the people and places that appear in *Wild Ivy*. I also benefited greatly while in the final stages of my work from advice generously given by Yoshizawa Katsuhiro, head of the translation bureau at the Institute for Zen Studies. Mr. Yoshizawa, who is engaged in producing a series of meticulously annotated editions of Hakuin's principal writings, was most generous in answering my questions, and unselfishly placed his work, much of it yet unpublished, at my disposal. Though possibly the first, I will certainly not be the last to appreciate his labors on what will, when it is completed, become the standard edition of Hakuin's works. It should provide the basis, and impetus, for the long overdue reappraisal of Hakuin's life and work that is to come. Finally, I wish to thank Ōtani University of Kyoto for aiding this publication with a generous grant.

Wild Ivy

1

Authentic Zen

THE DANGER OF FALSE TEACHINGS

NYONE WHO wants to achieve the Way of enlightenment must drive forward the wheel of the Four Great Vows. But even when you gain entry through the Gate of Nonduality, if you lack the Mind of Enlightenment, you will still sink back into the paths of evil.[1] In the past, the priest Tz'u-ming underwent great hardship while living and studying at Fen-yang. He made it his practice to always sit through the long nights, totally unmindful of the piercing cold found east of the river and never allowing himself so much as a wink of sleep. When the demon of sleep approached him, he would tell himself, "You pitiful wretch! What are you? If you're unable to utter a single word to benefit others while you live, when you die not a syllable you speak will be known to them," and jab himself in the thigh with a gimlet.[2] Here, truly, is a model to stand for a thousand future generations.

Anyone who would call himself a member of the Zen family must first of all achieve *kenshō*—realization of the Buddha's Way.[3] If a person who has not achieved kenshō says he is a follower of Zen, he is an outrageous fraud. A swindler pure and simple. A more shameless scoundrel than Kumasaka Chōhan.[4]

"The four great
universal vows
of a Bodhisattva"

It is commonly said that there are eight different schools of Buddhism in our land.[5] Doctrinal schools that devote themselves to mastering sutras and commentaries. Pure Land schools whose followers constantly recite the name of Amida Buddha. The Zen school—members of the Rinzai, Sōtō, and Ōbaku lineages—is regarded as being foremost among them all. In recent times, however, the Zen schools have been engaging in the practice of "silent illumination," doing nothing but sitting lifelessly like wooden blocks.[6] What, aside from that, do you suppose they consider their most urgent concern? Well, they witter on about being "men of nobility" who have "nothing at all to do." They proceed to live up to that self-proclaimed role. Consuming lots of good rice. Passing day after day in a state of seated sleep.[7] The surplice and cotton robe they wear as Buddhist priests is no more than a disguise. There's one old priest lives near here who just sits in his hermitage all day long, beating on the wooden fish and chanting in a loud voice, "*Namu kara taru nō. . . .*" True, there's a surplice hanging round his neck—but the man has never once experienced kenshō. I'd like to ask him: "What do the words '*tora ya ya*' that follow '*Namu kara taru nō*' really mean? I'll tell him what they mean: "Future existence is more terrifying than a hungry tiger!"[8] I have a verse that pours scorn on this odious race of pseudopriests:

> *Earth's vilest thing? From which all men recoil?*
> *Crumbly charcoal? Firewood that's wet? Watered lamp oil?*
> *A cartman? A boatman? A stepmother? Skunks?*
> *Mosquitoes? Lice? Blue flies? Rats? Thieving monks.*

Ahh! Monks! Priests! You can't all be thieves, every last one of you. And when I talk about thieving priests, I refer to those "silent illumination" Zennists who now infest the land.

Where our Zen school is concerned, anyone who achieves kenshō and leaves the house of birth-and-death is a house-leaver.

Not just someone who forsakes the family home and goes off to get his skull shaved. Still, you find people going around making unfounded claims: "I've left home, I'm a priest. I'm a priest." If that weren't bad enough, they then proceed to pocket the charity and donations they hoodwink laypeople, the householders, into giving them.[9]

Can anyone in the world support the tenuous thread of human existence without a home of some kind? Why do we use a special term like *layman? Layman*—a householder—is used in contrast to *priest*—a house-leaver. A layman's life is a precarious one—a hard and ceaseless struggle. Tilling the soil, plying a trade, running a shop, he is faced with almost constant adversity. He never has a moment's respite from the toils of birth-and-death. And so, from time to time, he offers donations to the priest, creating favorable karmic conditions that may enable him, in a future existence, to break free of birth-and-death.

For his part, the priest, in order to assist others to attain salvation, kindles a great burning faith in his heart. He opens the matchless eye of wisdom through the experience of kenshō, and then he works tirelessly to bestow the great gift of the Dharma, leading his fellow beings toward salvation in place of the Buddha patriarchs.

Priests and laity are thus like the wheels of a cart: they move forward in unison. But the sad assortment of today's priests we see spending their lives sitting like wood blocks in the complacent self-absorption of their "silent illumination" are incapable even of freeing themselves from birth-and-death. How can they possibly hope to assist laypeople to achieve a more favorable karma? Without giving so much as a thought to that, however, they freely and willingly accept donations from the lay community. Without a single scruple. I ask you, if they aren't thieves, what are they?

The day their parents sent them forth from their family homes to become Buddhist monks, little could they have dreamed their children would turn out to be the thieves you now see. It's all because of these counterfeit teachers with their plausible doctrines. They sink their hooks into people's fine, stalwart youngsters, and they turn them into a pack of blind and hairless dunces. The evil they wreak is truly immense. Blacker than the five great sins.[10] Preaching the Buddha's Dharma is a truly awesome responsibility. Something to be undertaken only with the greatest circumspection.

During the Shōtoku era [1711–1716], a young girl from a certain place in Tōtōmi Province died. Soon afterward, speaking through her younger sister, she described the horrible tortures she was undergoing in hell: "Hold a religious ceremony and maigre feast and recite the *Ten-Phrase Kannon Sutra* on my behalf," she said. "Save me from the dreadful heat of the Hell of Screams."[11]

Hearing her pleas, people said, "On the day of the funeral, when you were lying in your coffin, a priest of great virtue came and favored you by offering incense. What could have caused you to be reborn into such a terrible place?"

"Virtuous priest?" she replied. "What a lame joke that is. He and his endless talk of 'do-nothing silent illumination' Zen have led countless young sons and daughters to their ruin. Why, he himself fell into hell for his crimes. He is sure to stay here for a long, long time. He recently turned into a cow demon. Last time I saw him, he was pulling a blazing cart of fire. My ill-fated association with him was my undoing. Because of it, I, too, ended up in hell."

A great many people today have found themselves in situations similar to that young girl. You can read all about them in Suzuki Shōsan's *Tales of Cause and Effect.*[12]

At the beginning of the Kyōhō era [1716–1735], I was invited to a certain temple in the province of Kai.[13] A group of elder temple masters from surrounding areas came to lend their support. We sat far into the night, talking freely and openly about matters of the Way.

One of the priests, his voice sinking to a whisper, told us the following story: "An extraordinary thing has occurred not far from here. The priest of one of the important Shinto shrines in the province was possessed by a fox.[14] He offered prayers. He tried all the secret arts at his command. Nothing had any effect. It so happened that a nephew of his was the abbot of a Zen temple in Shinano Province, so a messenger was dispatched all the way to Shinano to give the nephew a full report of the misfortune that had befallen the uncle. The nephew was greatly alarmed by the news and set out immediately, traveling by fast litter, for the uncle's shrine.

"On arriving, he went directly to the afflicted man's room, his *shippei* [bamboo staff][15] grasped tightly in his fist. Standing before his uncle, he threw back his shoulders, braced himself, and with a fierce glower in his eye, roared out, 'Where did you come from, fox spirit! Begone! Leave this place at once. If you don't, I'll dispatch you with a blow from this staff.'

"'Do you know whom you are addressing?' the fox spirit replied. 'That *shippei* of yours couldn't even touch me. I am the high priest so-and-so, from such and such province.'

"Hearing the name that came from his uncle's lips, the nephew immediately laid his *shippei* on the floor and clasped his hands before him in veneration.

"'You were a great and good Buddhist teacher,' he said. 'What brought you such an ignominious retribution?'

"'Many years ago,' the fox spirit said, 'I made the mistake of preaching a false Dharma. Now I am paying for it.'

"'A false Dharma?' said the nephew. 'What do you mean?'

"'Do-nothing Unborn Zen. That (alas) was the false teaching.'[16]

"'But *unborn, undying*—those words appear in the Buddha's

6

sutras. How could that be such a terrible crime? The merit of expounding such a Dharma is extolled throughout the scriptures preached from the golden mouth of the Buddha himself. He said, "Even if you were to assemble every material benefit in the myriad-world universe and bestow it in charity to sentient beings, the virtue of that single phrase of Dharma teaching would still be greater by far." If sitting calm and undisturbed in the state of the Unborn were a transgression against the Dharma, wouldn't coughing, spitting, and moving your arms be transgressions as well?'

"'Preaching of the Dharma,' the fox spirit replied, 'must be undertaken with the greatest care. In the past, for the sin of uttering just two words—"Don't fall"—a priest fell into the body of a wild fox for five hundred lives.[17] The word *Unborn* is ten times worse than those two words. It takes hold of youths who have left their homes for the priesthood hungering to penetrate the Buddhist truth, and it saps their undoubting minds of all their fearlessness and vital spirit. One reason I am telling you all this is to atone for the sins I have committed. They still block my path to deliverance.'

"'How have you come here, honorable priest?' the nephew asked the fox spirit.

"'I am now Inari Myōjin,'[18] he answered. 'I have taken up residence at a shrine in the vicinity of the capital. I recently acquired the knack of flying through the air. I don't walk around on the ground much anymore because of the dogs—I find them a terrible nuisance.[19] I had to be in Edo for a short time to conduct some official business. On my way back home, I thought I'd have a look around the country. I landed here in Kai Province for a short stroll on the ground. The priest of that shrine caught sight of me and began throwing stones at me and berating me with some horrible abuse. Before I was aware what had happened, I had taken possession of him.'

7

"'No matter how much you torment him,' the priest said, 'it will do nothing to diminish the karma that is hindering you. Please, I beg you, release him and leave here. Focus your efforts at once on the task of exhausting your evil karma.'

"'An excellent idea,' said the fox spirit. 'You're right, of course. How true it is what they say about forgetting your past lives once you're reborn into a new existence.[20] I will do as you ask and release him.' Then he was gone.

"What a terrifying thing it is for a priest to preach an impure Dharma!"

"An extraordinary story," I said when the priest had finished his tale. "It should serve as an invaluable warning and lesson, particularly now, with the Zen school in such a dismal state of decline. But we must never disgrace the master who was reborn as the fox spirit by allowing his name to pass our lips. Think of his descendants. Can you imagine for a moment they would welcome, not be terribly saddened by, the news of his fate?"

The other priests just sat there with their hands clasped tightly together before them in earnest supplication. Some of their cheeks glistened with tears—but some of their brows were glistening with beads of sweat.[21]

> The sound of raindrops pattering on the fallen autumn leaves,
>   though sobering to the soul,
> Cannot compare to the splendid rich intimacy of sunset clouds
>   casting a warm glow over fields of yellowing grain.[22]

Tales from Childhood

Many years ago, when I was still a young child, my mother gave me a pat on the head. "Son," she said, counting off the days deliberately on her fingers, "you must always venerate the deity of the

Kitano Shrine. You were born on the twenty-fifth of the twelfth month in the second year of Jōkyō, at the first crow of the cock—two in the morning. The year, the month, the day, and the hour all fall under the sign of the ox. The twenty-fifth, as everyone knows, is the special day set aside to worship the Ox deity."[23]

So it seems I have some innate affinity with Kitano.

There was in those days a priest of the Nichiren sect by the name of Nichigon Shōnin.[24] He came from a place called Kubo-kane in Izu Province and was widely known for the unsurpassed power of his sermons. Nichigon held a lecture-meeting at the Shōgenkyō-ji, the local Nichiren temple in Hara. He took as his text the letters of Nichiren Shōnin.[25] People came from all around the village to hear him. They flocked in like clouds. I went with my mother, and we heard him describe in graphic detail the torments in each of the Eight Scorching Hells. He had every knee in the audience quaking, every liver in the house frozen stiff with fear. As little as I was, I was certainly no exception. My whole body shook in mortal terror.

When I went to bed that night, even in the security of my mother's bosom, my mind was in a terrible turmoil. I lay awake sobbing miserably all night, my eyes swollen with tears.

I recall one particular occasion when my mother took me into the bath. She liked to have the water in the tub boiling hot. She wasn't happy unless the servant girl constantly stoked the fire with more and more wood and fanned it up into a blazing inferno. Flames would rush madly up and around, shooting out like angry waves. The water seethed and churned in the tub, making low, rumbling groans like thunder, striking a panic of terror into me. I let out howls of distress of such force they nearly burst the bamboo bands off the water buckets.

People came running from all directions with looks of great alarm. They were sure something terrible had happened to me.

"Did you burn yourself?" "Is it the stomachache?" voices exclaimed. My only response was a torrential shed of tears.

Only one person was equal to the situation: my elder sister's husband—Maruya Hachirō—a man of unrivaled strength. He grabbed me up and barked into my ear, "If you're going to cry, at least let people know the reason why. Bawling away like that, you're worse than a little girl. Come now, tell me what's the matter."

"I'll tell mother. No one else," I blubbered. "Make all these other people go away."

When the last of them had gone out the back of the house, I kneeled down in front of my mother. Folding my arms sheepishly over my chest, I explained to her how the deep growling sounds from the bathtub had terrified me.

"I can't see what's so frightening about gurgling water," she said.

"Mother, you don't understand. I can't even go into the bath without having my knees knock and my blood run cold. Just think what it will be like when I have to face the burning fires of hell all by myself. What am I going to do? Isn't there any way to escape? Do I have to sit back and wait calmly until death comes? If you know something, please tell me about it. I want to know everything! Have pity on me. Save me. This intolerable agony continues day and night—I can't bear it any longer."

"Well, we can't discuss it in this dingy old bath," she said. "Tomorrow, let's find a place where it's nice and clean. I promise to tell you all you want to know about this important matter of yours."

I felt exuberant. I even got back into the tub again. The women pushed their way back into the room, still wanting to know the cause of my tears.

"No," mother told them, "this young man has something extremely important on his mind."

南無地獄大菩薩

"Homage to Hell,
the Great Bodhisattva"

"Look at his face!" they laughed. "As if nothing had happened . . . after all that fuss." Then, losing interest in the amusement, they went back to their work.

That night, I sank into a sound and blissful sleep. My eyes didn't open until well after eight o'clock the next morning, far past my usual hour for rising. I awoke to the clamor of youthful shouts coming from the grove of the Tenjin Shrine behind the house. A gang of children—my neighborhood playmates—were crying and screaming in a high pitch of excitement. I leaped out of bed and dashed out the door to see what they were up to. They had found some baby crows and were running about, jumping and hooting, trying to see who could strike the hardest blows at the young birds. I started forward, wanting to join the sport, then checked myself as my thoughts veered back to the house. Today, mother was supposed to divulge her great secret to me. That must come first. I turned on my heels and flew back into the house.

I found her having a leisurely chat with an elderly physician named Ichikawa Gendō. I went behind one of the sliding doors and sat, waiting for them to finish. After a while, Gendō appeared, said good-bye to my mother, and left.

I went up to her, pulling a sour face and scratching at my hair. "Mother," I said, "my hair is itchy. It feels very uncomfortable. I'm sorry to bother you, but would you please undo it and rebind it for me."

"My word!" she exclaimed, "what has got into you?"

Everyone within earshot came poking their heads in the door asking what had happened. "He says his hair feels itchy and makes him uncomfortable. He wants me to fix it for him," she answered.

"Next thing you know," they said, "the sun will be rising in the west."

Mother had a maidservant fetch the box with the combs in it. She took me to the edge of the room near the veranda. I told the servant girl she had to leave before we could start. She walked slowly out of the room, glancing curiously back over her shoulder.

When we were alone, I sat, kneeling properly in front of mother, and said, "Surely no one is as sinful as I am. Remember what you promised last night. If you know of some way to escape those burning hellfires, you must tell me and save me from this terrible distress."

"Son," she said, "you know I wouldn't keep anything from you. But let's do your hair first. We can attend to the other matter afterward."

"Tell me first," I objected. "Then you can do what you want with my hair. Please tell me first."

"No," she said, "first the hair."

We argued back and forth, then, as I stared hard into her eyes, it suddenly occurred to me: "She doesn't really know how to help me. Last night when she saw me sobbing uncontrollably, she told me a lie to get me to stop. Well, if that's her game, I'm going to throw another tantrum right now."

I jumped back, setting my jaw in readiness, but at that instant, she stopped me. "Wait a minute, young man. I'll tell you. It's this: You must always worship the deity of the Kitano Shrine."

Jubilant, I stretched my head forward so she could comb out my hair. As soon as she finished, I went to the altar room of our house, swept it clean, hung up a portrait of Tenjin, and placed some flowers on the altar. I then lit some incense and began to repeat the name of Tenjin over and over without letup. I had the *Tenjin Sutra* by heart that very night.[26] After that, I arose each night at the hour of the ox [about 2:00 AM], lit some incense, made my bows before Tenjin, and prayed for deliverance from the blazing conflagration that awaited me in hell.

My father became very angry at these goings-on. "You little idler. Up every night, wasting good lamp oil. A little fellow like you, reciting sutras. What good will it do you?"

"You, sir," interrupted my mother, "not only neglect your own religious duties; now you want to tell others not to perform theirs. It's a wonderful thing that your son wants to chant sutras. Don't try to stop him."

At that time, an archery game was enjoying a great vogue among young and old alike. It was played with small toy bows and arrows. Secretly, so as not to be found out, I decided to try my hand at target shooting. The sliding doors in our house, covered with paper printed in a chrysanthemum pattern, presented an inviting target. Determined to score a bull's-eye in one of those flowers, I gave myself up to the sport, forgetting all else.

There was a painting in our house, acquired by my elder brother, depicting the poet Saigyō standing under a willow tree. It was painted by an artist named Ryūi.[27] My brother treasured it and always kept it hanging in the *tokonoma*. Well, an arrow from my bow managed somehow or other to stray far from the mark. I shot a large hole right through Saigyō's left eye.

When I saw what I had done, my whole body began to tremble with fear. I pressed my palms together tightly before me and appealed to Tenjin to come to my rescue: "Great deity of Kitano. I place myself in your hands. Please, use your infinite compassion and the power of your marvelous vow to protect me. Keep this deed of mine from becoming known."

While I was sweating and squirming in distress, my brother, unknown to me, quietly returned home. He discovered the damaged painting, grabbed it down from the wall, and rushed with it into mother's room. He laid it in front of her and, with his face screwed up in anger, blustered, "See what that worthless little rascal of yours has gone and done now!" Then, composing himself a bit, he stalked from the room and banged out of the house, little caring where.

Mother looked thunder at me but made no attempt to scold me. I started blubbering away again. Inwardly, however, I was deeply shaken. "Ah, Tenjin," I thought, "you are a rather doubtful kind of deity. You can't even keep a relatively minor matter like this one covered up. How can I possibly rely on you to save me from the fires of hell?"

I left my bed again that night at the hour of the ox and set out my usual offerings of flowers and incense. I shut my eyes tightly, pressed my palms together before me, and said, "Great deity of Kitano, I place myself completely in your hands. If it is in your power to save me from the burning hellfires, please make the smoke from this incense rise up in a straight line. If you can't help me, make the smoke scatter."

I meditated for a time, my eyes closed, my hands still pressed tightly together. I opened my eyes. The smoke from the incense rose mercifully upward—straight as a string! Ah! I closed my eyes again, pondering my good fortune. This time when I opened them, my heart sank. The smoke was curling and scattering in all directions! My faith in Tenjin's power was badly shaken. I was a very unhappy young lad.

I had heard that when a person was in dire need of spiritual help such as I was, none of the Buddhist and Shinto deities could surpass the power possessed by the Bodhisattva Kannon. I promptly set about reciting the *Kannon Sutra*[28] and had it coming pat on my lips only a few nights later. I chanted it together with the *Tenjin Sutra* mornings and nights without fail.

Eventually, though, I began to reflect: "All these sutra recitations don't seem to be doing much good, despite all the time and effort I put into them. I still even dread it when I have moxa burned on my skin."

A troupe of puppeteers had arrived in the area and were performing at a place called Suwa. They were putting on a play titled *The Kettle Hat of Nisshin Shōnin.*[29] In it, Lord Tokimune, the regent at Kamakura, puts a question to the Nichiren priest

The deity
Tenjin

Nisshin: "Does a person who practices the teachings of the *Lotus Sutra* feel the heat of a burning fire?"

"A true practicer," replies Nisshin, "can enter a raging fire without being harmed. He can sink into the water without being drowned."

Lord Tokimune puts him to the test. A plowshare is heated in a fire and clamped around under Nisshin's arms. A red-hot cauldron is put over his head. Nisshin suffers through these tortures with complete equanimity. He even manages a smile.

The people in the audience were deeply impressed. By the play's end, they were chanting in unison choruses of the sacred title of the *Lotus Sutra*—"*Namu-myōhō-renge-kyō, Namu-myōhō-renge-kyō. . . .*"

The story started me thinking: "If one were a priest of Nisshin's caliber, it might even be possible to escape falling into the hellfires. I shall become a Buddhist priest. I shall become just like him."

I informed my mother of my desire to leave home for the priesthood as soon as possible.

"I find it wonderful how you are always so concerned about whether you will fall into hell or not," she said. "One way or another, it looks as if we're going to have to let you do what you want."

From then on, I devoted my days to the study of Buddhist sutras. I also read through a Zen anthology of poetical phrases.[30] It took me two months: I started it on the twenty-fifth of the ninth month, the eleventh year of Genroku [1698], and finished on the twenty-fifth of the eleventh month. Here again, my affinity with Kitano showed itself.

ORDINATION AND RELIGIOUS LIFE

I went to the Shōin-ji and became a monk at the age of fourteen. Beginning that very same spring, I began serving as an attendant of Nyoka Rōshi.[31] During this period, I read my way through the Five Confucian Classics and studied the literary anthology *Wen-hsüan* from cover to cover.[32] When I turned eighteen, I accompanied Kin Shuso to the city of Shimizu,[33] where we were admitted to the assembly of monks at the Zensō-ji. In the course of one of the lectures there, the story of Yen-t'ou the Ferryman came up. Wanting to learn more about the life of this priest, I got hold of a copy of *Praise of the True School,*[34] and Kin and I read through it on our own. I learned that Yen-t'ou had met a violent death at the hands of bandits.

It was a very disheartening discovery. After all, Yen-t'ou was said to be the kind of person who comes along only once in five hundred years: he was truly one of the dragons of his age. If it were possible for such a man to be assaulted and killed by common bandits while he was still alive, how could an ordinary garden-variety monk like me hope to avoid falling into the three evil paths[35] after I died? A Buddhist monk, I concluded, had to be the most useless creature on the face of the earth.

"What manner of divine punishment is being visited upon me! How I rue the day I let them shave my hair off with that razor! Look at me! A sorry, wretched-looking outcast. I can't possibly return to lay life—I'd be too ashamed. And it would be just as humiliating to sneak off somewhere and fling myself to a watery grave. One thing is sure, I am at the end of my religious quest. What a total, miserable failure I've become."

For a full three days, I lay tossing restlessly on my bedding, tormented by these thoughts. I began to waste away right there in the monks' quarters. Not so much as a grain of rice would pass my craving throat.

Fifteen unbearable days, and through it all, I could not for the life of me drive those burning hellfires from my mind. Brooding, pondering my future over and over, cudgeling my brain for some answer, I finally came to the conclusion that, since there seemed to be no way at all to avoid entering the three paths and hell in the next life, I might as well join hands and take the leap into the conflagration along with everyone else.

At the same time, I could see no point in just wasting the rest of my life. I decided I would turn my attention to the study of calligraphy and the composition of Chinese poetry. I would try to earn universal praise as one of the master artists of the age. The matter of my future existence could take its own course. I began to familiarize myself with the major writers of the T'ang period—Li Po, Tu Fu, Han Yü, and Liu Tsung-yüan. In calligraphy, I studied the models of Sōnen and Yōsetsu.[36]

The following year, I set out on a pilgrimage to southern Mino Province, drawn by stories of a man named Baō Rōjin, incumbent of the Zuiun-ji in a village called Hino, northwest of Ōgaki Castle.[37]

According to the reports, no one in the present day could compare with him in the field of poetry and letters. I traveled in a group with twelve other monks. On arriving at Zuiun-ji, we requested permission to stay and took up residence that same day in Baō's temple.

Zuiun-ji was incomparably poor. Students even had to supply their own rice and firewood. As for Baō, who was known as the "Wild Horse of Mino," he was by nature hard and sharp as flint, rough and ruthless to the core—as forbidding as they come. He spewed his venom wholesale: everyone received an equal dose regardless of rank or ability. As a result of this, the monks I had come with were all soon anxious to leave and escape the old man. They decided to break up and go their separate ways.

I was alone in my belief that another teacher with Baō's wide learning would be hard to find, even were I to search the entire country. As for his severity, I wasn't going to let that frighten me off. What rice and firewood I needed, and even luxuries such as *miso* and *shoyu*, I could manage out of my travel money—a gift

19

from my mother that I still held in reserve. Whatever happened, I felt there was little cause for worry. I vowed to myself that I was not going to leave my newfound teacher, even if it should turn out to be the death of me.

As the other monks were hurrying about readying their travel packs, yelling and calling out to one another in high spirits, I was off by myself, squatting down next to the well busy washing some radishes. I was unaware that Baō had come up behind me until I heard him speak: "Crane, Crane [*Kaku*] . . . the young birds are flying off in fine feather, aren't they?"[38]

From then on, through fair and foul, it was just the two of us. Whenever it wasn't actually raining, Baō would be off enjoying himself in Ōgaki. Because of this, people around the temple would refer to a cloudless day as "a Baō sky."[39] I would stay behind in the temple and devote myself quietly to my reading. There was a man named Onbazan, Baō's sole disciple at the time and a poet of some reputation, who would drop over from time to time and help me with the composition of linked verse.[40] We would start off our sessions by composing a hundred lines between us, Onbazan doing the first line, I matching it. It never took long to accomplish this—about the time for a couple of sticks of incense to burn down.[41]

One day, I was alone in the temple turning things over in my head. It suddenly dawned on me that even in the unlikely event I attained a skill at writing verse that surpassed the likes of a Li Po or Tu Fu, it still wouldn't help me avoid falling into the three evil paths when I died. I sank once again into a very melancholy state—sadly regretting the situation in which I found myself.

My gaze happened to turn to the far end of the veranda, where several hundred old books had been stacked, after an airing, on top of an old writing desk. The moment I saw them, I experienced an indescribable surge of joy. I promptly lit some incense and recited a sutra. Then I made three deep bows, and vowed: "All Buddhas in the ten directions. All the gods who stand guard over the Dharma. I place my trust in you. If a way exists to which I can devote the rest of my life, I entreat you to make it known to me."

Quietly approaching the desk and shutting my eyes, I stretched out my hand and blindly picked up one of the volumes. I raised it up several times in reverence, then lifted my eyelids. I had chosen a great treasure—*Spurring Students through the Zen Barrier!*[42]

Almost beside myself with joy, I opened it carefully and scanned the words printed on the page before me. I had turned to a passage that described the great hardships the Chinese priest Tz'u-ming underwent many years ago while he was studying under Zen master Fen-yang.

ZEN PILGRIMAGE

The following year, I moved on to the Hofuku-ji in Horado and joined the assembly under Nanzen Oshō.[43] Nanzen had composed a verse to celebrate the New Year. When I saw it, I immediately composed one of my own, employing the same rhyme scheme:

> *Brandishing the Taia Sword, a fistful of frost,*
> *He summons springtime back throughout the world;*
> *An auspicious light suffuses the abbot's chamber,*
> *Old Mr. South, offering incense for the New Year.*[44]

I presented this verse to Baō when I returned to the Zuiun-ji. He laughed and said, "Your position in the brotherhood is sure to rise by the time of the summer retreat."[45]

21

Baō's prediction turned out to be accurate. There were sixty men in Nanzen's assembly; by the end of the year, I had advanced to the rank of third senior monk. I was twenty-one years old.

In the spring of the next year, my younger brother in the Dharma, a monk named Eshō (he was later known as Kairyō and resided at the Genryū-ji), showed up at the Zuiun-ji.[46] He had found me there by tracing, step by step, the path that had brought me to the temple. He arrived without a cent of travel money to his name. The Zuiun-ji was, as I have said, poor in the extreme, so there was no question of allowing him to stay. The best that could be done was to arrange for him to be put up temporarily at a nearby temple.

Meantime, I traveled to Obama in Wakasa Province to attend a lecture-meeting on the *Record of Hsi-keng* being given by Master Banri.[47] I was able to renew some old acquaintances while I was there and also to ask whether anyone had knowledge of a temple where a penniless monk might be allowed to practice. One of the monks, who said that he was unaware of any such place nearby, suggested the Shōjū-ji, a temple in Matsuyama, Iyo Province. The lands around Matsuyama Castle were extremely fertile and the people prosperous, a situation highly favorable for a monk with an empty purse, who could provide for his needs by donations he received from begging. When I returned to the Zuiun-ji, I talked Eshō into going with me to Shikoku. We went and took up residence in the Monks Hall of the Shōjū-ji.[48]

During our stay in Matsuyama, rumors about the monks visiting the temple that summer being men of wide learning reached the ears of a high-ranking military retainer, a man whose family had served the local ruling clan for generations. He invited five monks from the Shōjū-ji to visit him at his residence for a chat over tea. I was one of the monks selected to go.

When the day came, we proceeded to his residence, and after exchanging words of introduction and small talk about the weather, our host brought out a collection of hanging scrolls to show us. There were about twenty scrolls, including calligraphy inscriptions, some of which our host confessed he was unable to decipher. Hearing that, the other monks all looked in my direction, their faces wreathed in broad grins.

There was one scroll in particular, an inscription in which the strokes of the characters were improperly written. No matter which way you read them, it was impossible to make out what the inscription said. While the others sat there with puckered brows, scratching their heads in bafflement, I took the scroll and wrote on the back of it the characters for "mother-in-law" and "old woman." Their brows now furrowed into frowns. Their fists clenched tightly at their sides.

"Now what does that mean?" muttered one. "That's very difficult to understand, too," another mumbled. "Can't make it out at all," said a third. "Please, elder monk," they said to me, "get off your perch in the absolute. Come down into our relative world and tell us what it says."

So, "descending below the clouds," I let them in on my little joke. "Those two characters mean: 'difficult . . . to . . . read. . . .'" They responded in loud honks of laughter and much clapping of hands.[49]

There was one scroll that was nested in a set of double wooden boxes. This was encased in turn within a bag of fine silk brocade. We watched with a mixture of wonder and reverence as the scroll was carefully taken out for our inspection. It was a piece of calligraphy by Daigu Sōchiku.[50] His vigorous brush strokes and the words he had chosen both seemed altogether fitting and natural. Everything about it was just as it should be. I thought to myself: This is the product of truly enlightened activity. that calligraphy meant far more to me than any of the other scrolls—my interest in which now immediately vanished.

As soon as I got back to the temple, I went to my quarters

23

and assembled my small collection of inscriptions and paintings—
about a score in all—some copybooks of calligraphy that had been
made for me, drawings and calligraphy others had done at my
request (which I had always treasured), as well as a few specimens
of my own brushwork. Bundling them up, I took them out into
the cemetery, put them in front of one of the egg-shaped tomb-
stones, and set fire to them. I watched until they were completely
consumed by the flames.

CROSSING THE THRESHOLD

From then on, I took *Spurring Students through the Zen Barrier* as
my master. Rededicated to my practice, I began pushing myself
mercilessly day and night. While reading the *Three Teachings of
the Buddha Patriarchs*,[51] I came upon a passage that made me leap
up with joy. It compared a student practicing the Great Vehicle
to a log floating down a river: never touching at either bank, it
finally makes its way out into the great ocean.

In the spring, at the urging of a former brother-monk, I
traveled to Fukuyama and joined the brotherhood at the Tenshō-
ji. There, by virtue of hard and continuous application to my
practice, I entered a pitch-dark cave. When I walked around or
engaged in other activities, I wasn't even aware of what I was
doing.[52] When autumn came, I set out for home with a party of
my fellow monks.

We skirted the shores of the Inland Sea at Maiko, over the
beaches of Suma. We passed the burial mound of the poet Hito-
maru and the grave of Atsumori. We walked through the fields
of Koyano and beside the woods of Ikuta.[53] But my eyes were not
open to any of those famous sights. All the way home, it seemed
as if I were not moving at all but standing in the road alone, and

the people, houses, and trees that lined the way were all moving westward.

It took about a fortnight to reach home. My family, relatives, and friends all gathered to welcome me. They were anxious to hear me tell them tales of everything, good and bad, I had experienced during my absence. But all they got for their questions was an unresponsive series of sublingual grunts: "Uh . . . Uh . . ." This bewildered them. They accused me of having somehow changed. They told me that I had become a "strange fellow."

But my behavior at this time was perfectly in keeping with that described in traditional accounts of other Zen practicers passed down through the centuries. The National Master Kanzan, for example, is said to have walked the entire length of the Great Eastern Road twenty times without once looking up to notice Mount Fuji as he passed beneath it.[54] I still remember the deep impression that story made on me when I first heard it. It filled me with an admiration for Master Kanzan that has never diminished.

Some time after that, I came upon a passage in *Spurring Students through the Zen Barrier* about the Bodhisattva Ever-Weeping. He was addressed by a voice, arising from nowhere, telling him not to look to the right or left, not to turn his gaze up or down, or in any of the four directions, as he walked along. I have trusted in those words ever since,[55] have treated them as a koan. Perhaps that's why I've turned into such a foolish fellow!

It was around that same time that I heard reports of a Zen monk in Echigo Province who had received Dharma sanction [*inka*] from the Ōbaku master Egoku Dōmyō.[56] A series of lectures on *The Eye of Men and Gods* was to be held soon at the Eigan-ji in Echigo. Availing myself of that opportunity, when spring came, I got three other monks to accompany me to the city of Takada to attend the meeting. The first thing I did on arriving was to seek out the monk I had heard about. We had a long discussion, which gave me an opportunity to observe in detail the depth of his understanding. I realized he was not the enlightened man he had been made out to be.

Disappointed, I hid myself inside a shrine room dedicated to the lords of the province, vowing to fast and concentrate single-mindedly on my practice for a period of seven days. No one in the temple knew where I was or what I was doing, not even the monks I had come with. Unable to find me, they assumed I had left secretly for home.

At around midnight on the seventh and final night of my practice, the boom of a bell from a distant temple reached my ears: suddenly, my body and mind dropped completely away. I rose clear of even the finest dust. Overwhelmed with joy, I hollered out at the top of my lungs, "Old Yen-t'ou is alive and well!"[57]

My yells brought my companions running from the monks' quarters. We joined hands, and they shared with me the intense joy of the moment. After that, however, I became extremely proud and arrogant. Everyone I encountered seemed to me like so many lumps of dirt.

Five hundred monks had gathered to take part in the lecture-meeting. As the regular residence hall was small in the extreme, the main hall of the neighboring Sōtō temple was borrowed and put to use as a detached residence. I was named senior monk and placed in charge of a group of thirty men that was sent from the main temple to be quartered in the hall. Among them were seven or eight of my comrades. One of them, a monk named Dan Zennin (later known as Kyōsui Oshō, he served as resident priest of the Rinzai-ji) who acted as my assistant,[58] came scurrying back from the main temple in a state of high excitement. "An extraordinary new monk has just arrived," he told us. "He is well over six feet tall and has a menacing look on his face. He planted himself in the entrance with a gigantic staff under his arm. Just stood there straight and motionless, like a great, with-

Yen-t'ou the Ferryman

ered tree, calling out for permission to stay in the rough, booming accents of the Bandō region.[59] I can tell you, he's no ordinary monk. I don't know if it's wise to let someone like that stay here." Undisguised signs of disapproval showed on the faces of the other monks as well.

Shortly after that, Dan came scurrying back again. "They held a discussion back at the main temple," he blurted out excitedly. "They decided to send him over here to us. They seem to think this is some sort of dumping ground for all their misfits and troublemakers."[60]

I scolded Dan: "Why are you running back and forth like this circulating bits of gossip you pick up? You're distracting your fellow monks from their practice! Why don't you take a look at *The Eye of Men and Gods* and prepare yourself for the lecture?"

Just then, Chō Jōza, the senior monk from the main temple (the person I had traveled to Echigo to meet), appeared at the detached residence, bringing the new arrival with him. He announced in an earnest and obliging manner, "This new monk is from Shinano Province. He will stay here with you in the annex. We've placed him at the bottom of the monks' roster. We request that you afford him the benefit of your guidance and assign him some task such as sweeping or cleaning."

"I don't understand why you brought him here," I said. "We already have six or seven monks staying here who are notorious for causing disturbances in training halls. This building isn't even ours. We borrowed it from a Sōtō temple. Don't you think it would be better to put serious-minded students here? That fellow may look well-mannered to you now, but when he finds out what those others are like, there's going to be hell to pay. He's a rogue monk. A real troublemaker."

"We sent him here because we thought we could count on you to handle him," said the head monk.

"In that case," I replied, "we must bow to your decision. But at the first sign of any irregular behavior, he goes right back to you. Is that agreed?"

He gave his unqualified assurance that there would be no objection to my condition. That settled things, and he returned to the main temple.

The next day, the opening of the lecture-meeting went off without a hitch. Senior priests went around the Monks Hall congratulating the men. Chō Jōza came over from the main temple to pay his respects as well. While he was there, he picked up a copy of *The Eye of Men and Gods* that he saw lying nearby. Flipping some pages, he pointed out several places in the text and addressed questions to some of the monks around him.

"What is your interpretation of this passage?" he asked one.

"How about here? How do you explain this?" he asked another.

When he had finished examining them in this way, he left. After he was gone, the new monk said, "Was that the senior monk?"

"What business is it of yours?" I replied.

"I admit what he said showed some insight," the monk replied. "But his understanding of that one passage certainly wasn't sound."

I challenged him to say something about a few of the passages himself. He proceeded to explain them one by one, in a way that showed great discernment and clarity.

The judgment that the monks in the hall had formed of the man (who turned out to be called Kaku; he was a student of a priest named Shōju)[61] underwent an abrupt and radical change. They now sat in hushed silence, trembling apprehensively. Some other monks who had been hanging around the hall freely dispensing their personal views and opinions seemed to suffer a sudden attack of timidity as well. I didn't see their faces after that.

To me, he was like a fresh rain after a long drought. I felt as though I had met an old and trusted friend from my native village. From then on, we spent our days and nights debating matters of the Dharma. I could not have wished for a greater pleasure.

The evening of the final lecture arrived all too soon, and it was time for us to leave. I invited Kaku to meet me privately so I could ask him about his teacher.

"He's an old hermit named Etan Zōsu. He lives at the Shōju-an, a hermitage in Iiyama," he told me.[62]

I secretly yearned to go to Iiyama and pay my respects to the old man.

"Just what I was hoping you would propose," Kaku replied when I asked him what he thought of the idea. "If you go, I'll go along with you."

The next day, we waited for the bell to announce the close of the meeting, then we slipped unnoticed out the temple gate. We made our way up over the pass at Mount Tomikura and from there proceeded directly on to Iiyama.

SHŌJU RŌJIN

When we arrived at the Shōju-an hermitage, I received permission to be admitted as a student, then hung up my traveling staff to stay.

Once, after I had set forth my understanding to the master during *dokusan* [personal interview], he said to me, "Commitment to the study of Zen must be genuine. How do you understand the koan about the Dog and the Buddha-Nature?"[63]

"No way to lay a hand or foot on that," I replied.

He abruptly reached out and caught my nose. Giving it a sharp push with his hand, he said, "Got a pretty good hand on it there!"

Shōju Rōjin

I couldn't make a single move, either forward or backward. I was unable to spit out a single syllable.

That encounter put me into a very troubled state. I was totally frustrated and demoralized. I sat red-eyed and miserable, my cheeks burning from the constant tears.

The master took pity on me and assigned me some koans to work on: Su-shan's Memorial Tower, The Water Buffalo Comes through the Window, Nan-ch'üan's Death, Nan-ch'üan's Flowering Shrub, The Hemp Robe of Ching-chou, Yün-men's Dried Stick of Shit.[64]

"Anyone who gets past one of these fully deserves to be called a descendant of the Buddhas and patriarchs," he said.

A great surge of spirit rose up inside me, stiffening my resolve. I chewed on those koans day and night. Attacking them from the front. Gnawing at them from the sides. But not the first glimmer of understanding came. Tearful and dejected, I sobbed out a vow: "I call upon the evil kings of the ten directions and all the other leaders of the heavenly host of demons. If after seven days I fail to bore through one of these koans, come quickly and snatch my life away."

I lit some incense, made my bows, and resumed my practice. I kept at it without stopping for even a moment's sleep. The master came and spewed abuse at me. "You're doing Zen down in a hole!" he barked.

Then he told me, "You could go out today and scour the entire world looking for a true teacher—someone who could revive the fortunes of 'closed-barrier' Zen—you'd have a better chance finding stars in the midday skies."[65]

I had my doubts about that. "After all," I reasoned, "there are great monasteries all over the country that are filled with celebrated masters: they're as numerous as sesame or flax seed. That old man in his wretched ramshackle old poorhouse of a temple—

and that preposterous pride of his! I'd be better off leaving here and going somewhere else."

Early the next morning, still deeply dejected, I picked up my begging bowl and went into the village below Iiyama Castle.

I was totally absorbed in my koan—never away from it for an instant. I took up a position beside the gate of a house, my bowl in my hand, fixed in a kind of trance. From inside the house, a voice yelled out, "Get away from here! Go somewhere else!" I was so preoccupied, I didn't even notice it. This must have angered the occupant, because suddenly she appeared flourishing a broom upside down in her hands. She flew at me, flailing wildly, whacking away at my head as if she were bent on dashing my brains out. My sedge hat lay in tatters. I was knocked over and ended heels up on the ground, totally unconscious. I lay there like a dead man.[66]

Neighbors, alarmed by the commotion, emerged from their houses with looks of concern on their faces. "Oh, now look what the crazy old crone has done," they cried, and quickly vanished behind locked doors. This was followed by a hushed silence; not a stir or sign of life anywhere. A few people who happened to be passing by approached me in wonderment. They grabbed hold of me and hoisted me upright.

"What's wrong?" "What happened?" they exclaimed.

As I came to and my eyes opened, I found that the unsolvable and impenetrable koans I had been working on—all those venomous cat's-paws—were now penetrated completely. Right to their roots. They had suddenly ceased to exist. I began clapping my hands and whooping with glee, frightening the people who had gathered around to help me.

"He's lost his mind!" "A crazy monk!" they shouted, shrinking back from me apprehensively. Then they turned heel and fled, without looking back.

I picked myself up from the ground, straightened my robe,

33

and fixed the remnants of my hat back on my head. With a blissful smile on my face, I started, slowly and exultantly, making my way back toward Narasawa and the Shōju-an.[67]

I spotted an old man beckoning to me. "Honorable priest," he said, addressing me, "that old lady really put your lights out, didn't she?"

I smiled faintly but uttered not a word in response. He gave me a bowl of rice to eat and sent me on my way.

I reached the gate of Shōju's hermitage with a broad grin on my face. The master was standing on the veranda. He took one look at me and said, "Something good has happened to you. Try to tell me about it."

I walked up to where he was standing and proceeded to explain at some length about the realization I had experienced. He took his fan and stroked my back with it.

"I sincerely hope you live to be my age," he said. "You must firmly resolve you will never be satisfied with trifling gains. Now you must devote your efforts to post-satori training. People who remain satisfied with a small attainment never advance beyond the stage of the Shravakas. Anyone who remains ignorant of the practice that comes after satori will invariably end up as one of those unfortunate Arhats of the Lesser Vehicle. Their rewards are paltry indeed. Why, I'd rather you be reborn into the mangy, suppurating body of an old fox than for you ever to become a priest of the Two Vehicles."[68]

By post-satori training, he means going forward after your first satori and devoting yourself to continued practice—and when that practice bears fruit, to continue on still further. As you keep on proceeding forward, you will arrive at some final, difficult barriers.[69]

What is required is simply "continuous and unremitting devotion to hidden practice, scrupulous application—that is the essence within the essence."[70] The bands of Unborn Zennists you run into nowadays, sitting like withered tree stumps "silently illuminating" themselves, are an even worse lot than those hateful, suppurating old foxes.

"What is 'hidden practice and scrupulous application'?" someone asked.

It certainly doesn't mean sneaking off to some mountain and sitting like a block of wood on a rock or under a tree "silently illuminating" yourself. It means immersing yourself totally in your practice at all times and in all your daily activities—walking, standing, sitting, or lying down. Hence, it is said that practice concentrated in activity is a hundred, a thousand, even a million times superior to practice done in a state of inactivity.[71]

Upon attaining satori, if you continue to devote yourself to your practice single-mindedly, extracting the poison fangs and talons of the Dharma cave, tearing the vicious, life-robbing talismans into shreds,[72] combing through texts of all kinds, Buddhist and non-Buddhist alike, accumulating a great store of Dharma wealth, whipping forward the wheel of the Four Universal Vows, pledging yourself to benefit and save all sentient beings while striving every minute of your life to practice the great Dharma giving, and having nothing—nothing—to do with fame or profit in any shape or form—you will then be a true and legitimate descendant of the Buddha patriarchs. It's a greater reward than gaining rebirth as a human or a god.

"What about the saying that worldly fortune is a curse in the three periods?"[73]

Great numbers of men and women seek advantageous rebirth in the next life, wanting to achieve Buddhahood, wanting to be born into the Pure Land. They strictly observe a life of purity. Uphold the precepts to the letter. Recite and copy sutras over and over. Hold services for the Buddhas, extend charity to the priesthood, worshiping them with deep bows of reverence. Make pilgrimages to religious centers throughout the land: to

"Practice concentrated in activity is a hundred, a thousand, even a million times superior to practice done in a state of inactivity"

Chichibu in Bandō, to Shikoku in western Japan, to Nara, and Mount Kōya. People perform good works by the thousands, availing themselves of every secret art known to man—and yet as long as they don't attain the Way by experiencing kenshō and hearing the sound of the single hand,[74] they still aren't close to Buddhahood: they'll never even glimpse the Pure Land. What the world regards as good and beneficial is a bane in the three periods.

How about your present existence? By enduring endless hardships and performing countless good deeds, you may be assured of rebirth in your next existence as a prince, a gallant general, a powerful lord, perhaps the head of some distinguished family. Then you will have riches and rank to use at will. Power at your fingertips. You will no doubt exult in all that wealth and power. In this new existence, the events of your prior life will be totally forgotten. All those numberless acts of goodness performed in your former life will have vanished like dewdrops in the sun. You will gather an assortment of beautiful women for your wives, nubile concubines to embrace. Servants and vassals at your beck and call in numbers you cannot even count. There will be fine purple skirts for wife Chang. Stockings of precious gauze for concubine Li. The coffers of your own treasury not being equal to such extravagances, you will covet the property of others, engage in wholesale plunder, squeezing the people till they are dry, grinding the poor to powder. These acts of oppression will cause your subjects untold suffering.

Piling evil deeds one on top of the other in such abundance, you will undoubtedly head straight for the evil destinations when you die. You will fall into one of the three evil paths, where an endless round of torment and suffering awaits you, or be born into one of the eight difficult realms.[75] In the face of this, could anyone deny that worldly fortune is a curse in the three periods?

A monk standing nearby said, "But surely worldly fortune is

only a problem for laypeople. It wouldn't apply once you enter the priesthood."

Indeed, it does, I replied. It does, but that's a subject I'm reluctant to enter into here. It would involve telling stories about other priests.

"Then how can a priest avoid the evil caused by worldly fortune?" he asked.

To begin with, I said, he must achieve kenshō—see into his own nature—and attain the Way. If he wants to see his nature, he must first "hear the sound of the single hand." And even when he hears it, he must not be satisfied. Next he must "put a stop to all sounds,"[76] and then he must pass, one by one, all the other unsolvable, impassable koans. Even then, a final, difficult barrier remains.

"But after kenshō is attained and you have entered the path of enlightenment," he said, "surely there's no evil to obstruct you then?"

Indeed, there is! It exists if you create it. If you don't create it, it doesn't exist. But such distinctions can wait until after you've attained the Way. You can pose such questions to yourself then—it won't be too late.

Of particular importance are the three kinds of succession.[77] That is a distinction you should be aware of.

"Would you tell me about them?" he asked.

One of the ancients said that a superior man succeeds his enemy, a man of average ability succeeds his benefactor, and an inferior man succeeds a figure of authority.

The "enemy" is he whose rigorous scoldings and stinging fists rob you of your heart, liver, and all your other vital organs. What is he if not your enemy?

The benefactor and the figure of authority need no special comment. Even here among the students under my own mallet, a great many of the average and inferior types are to be found.

I'm to blame for it. It's my shortcoming, my transgression, not theirs. If I had the strength to push them, don't think they would sweetly submit to being average or inferior. There are some who will succeed their benefactors because the teachers who raised and educated them will tell them to do so, and they will be unable to refuse.

Take my own case. One day, when I was in Iiyama with old Shōju, he summoned me. "I know this mountain hermitage is a very poor place," he said. "But in the future, when I have left on my final pilgrimage, I want you to come and live out the rest of your days here."

"You are fortunate in already having a senior monk like Kaku," I replied.

His answer to this was: "I can't depend on him."

At the time, the significance of this remark was lost on me. It seemed a strange thing for him to say. Not too many years after that, when Kaku suddenly passed away, I realized for the first time the tremendous penetration of old Shōju's eye.[78] It's a shame I did not succeed my enemy and become a superior man!

THE MIND OF ENLIGHTENMENT

What is to be valued above all else is the practice that comes after satori is achieved. What is that practice? It is practice that puts the Mind of Enlightenment first and foremost.

Many years ago, the great deity of the Kasuga Shrine appeared to Gedatsu Shōnin of Kasagi.[79] "Since the time of the Buddha Kuruson," he told him, "every wise and eminent priest who has lacked the Mind of Enlightenment has without exception fallen into the paths of evil."

For years, these words weighed on my mind, greatly troubling me. I couldn't understand it. Wasn't a shaven head and monk's robe the Mind of Enlightenment? Wasn't reciting sutras, mantras, and dharanis the Mind of Enlightenment? Not to mention all those wise and eminent priests throughout the past: the idea that such men could have lacked the Mind of Enlightenment seemed incomprehensible to me. Yet here was a sacred utterance from the august lips of the great deity of Kasuga. It certainly could not be dismissed lightly.

I first began to have these doubts when I was twenty-five. They remained with me until my forty-first year, when I at long last penetrated into the heart of this great matter. Suddenly, unexpectedly, I saw it—it was as clear as if it were right there in the hollow of my hand. What is the Mind of Enlightenment? It is, I realized, a matter of doing good—benefiting others by giving them the gift of the Dharma teaching.

I pledged that I would from that moment forth drive forward the wheel of the Four Great Universal Vows. Now I am more than eighty years of age, but I have never been remiss in my effort to fulfill that pledge. I go wherever I am asked. Fifty, a hundred leagues—it doesn't faze me in the least. I do everything I possibly can to impart the Dharma to people. How strange it is that nowhere in the Buddhist teachings or in the records of the Zen patriarchs have I seen any clarification of the Mind of Enlightenment. How fortunate it was for me that the great deity of Kasuga, in an oracle of a few short sentences, succeeded so wonderfully in transcending all the sutras and commentaries. My joy could not have been any greater.

Now, without regard for any slips my writing brush may make, I will just jot down the essentials of Gedatsu Shōnin's story. It will perhaps serve as a small Dharma gift arising out of the Mind of Enlightenment.

Many years ago, when Myōe Shōnin was at Toganōō in seclusion from the world[80] and Gedatsu Shōnin was residing at his temple on Mount Kasagi, the two men visited the Kasuga Shrine in Nara from time to time to perform services on behalf of the Kasuga deity. When Myōe came to the shrine, the deity opened the doors to the shrine's inner sanctuary and engaged him in pure, spiritual discourse extending over all the Buddhist sutras and commentaries.

When Gedatsu appeared, the doors opened for him, too, but the deity had his back turned and did not engage Gedatsu in spiritual dialogue. Gedatsu was sad but at the same time baffled. "Is there any difference between my learning or religious practice and Myōe's?" he asked. "Whereas you deign to talk with Myōe whenever he comes, you turn your back on me. What does it mean? Is it not counter to the vow you yourself have made—to extend your benefits universally and save all beings?"

The deity addressed Gedatsu in a loud and noble voice of great sublimity. "It is because of your achievements in learning that you are able to see my back. Your lack of the Mind of Enlightenment has been a constant disappointment to me," he said. He then reascended into the heavens.

Gedatsu, sad and despondent, rose and left the shrine. Back home in his room at Kasagi, he continued reading far into the night, holding a lamp up for light, until everyone else had retired. He was alone, surrounded by total stillness. All at once, the silence was broken by sounds of a great commotion outside the room. Summoning up his courage, Gedatsu approached the window, his body rigid with fear. He poked a small hole in the paper window with his finger and peered out into the darkness.

Terrifying apparitions, specter shapes with cowlike heads and horselike faces, were milling about in confusion, madly snapping and lunging and grabbing at one another in a wild frenzy of excitement. It was like a scene of agony and suffering from the realm of fighting demons.

Gedatsu's whole body shook uncontrollably with fear; cold shivers shot up and down his spine; his hair stood on end. He

Kannon
Bodhisattva

then noticed that an aged monk was standing next to him in a solemn trance. He spoke to him through trembling lips: "What are those monstrous creatures out there?"

The old monk spoke: "Those depraved, fiendish beings? Ah! You can be sure they are up to no good. It is a serious transgression even to talk about them. But since you have asked, it can't be helped. I must tell you their story.

"Those beings were all once wise and celebrated priests who lived after the time of the Buddha Kuruson. Because they did not possess the Mind of Enlightenment, they fell into the evil paths. They are all perfectly well known, yet it would be a terrible wrong on my part to tell you who they are.

"A person may practice hard, practice assiduously, and keep at it even until Maitreya Buddha comes to earth far in the future. He may attain great enlightenment, acquire vast stores of knowledge and wisdom so that he excels countless millions of his fellow seekers. And yet, for all that, if he fails to encounter a clear-minded teacher, he will never come to learn about post-satori practice—much less will he discover the precious Mind of Enlightenment.

"Those demons are always there, both day and night, biding their time, seeking their chance. For they mean to have you in there with them. Even for those demons, it will be no easy task to make you one of their number. Because, in the past, you have from time to time shown sparks of sympathy and compassion in offering religious guidance to younger students. I expect, however, that you may find yourself drawn in among them anyway, before too long."

"Where are you from, good priest?" Gedatsu asked. "I haven't seen you here before."

"I live close by," he replied, "near the fields of Kasuga. I've come on your account. But it would not be advisable to remain here much longer. When dawn comes, it would be unseemly for me to be seen talking with you like this. I will say farewell to you now."

With that, he mounted a white cloud and flew off in the direction of Kasuga, leaving Gedatsu filled with a boundless sense of gratitude.

About that time, several of the monks I had parted company with back at the Eigan-ji showed up in Iiyama looking for me. They wanted me to return home with them to Shōin-ji. If I refused to go, they said, they would remain in Iiyama with me. While I was debating what to do, unable to arrive at a decision, a letter arrived from home informing me that Nyoka Rōshi had taken ill and was confined to his bed. I was much dismayed and saddened by the news and decided to set out for home without delay. The three monks, who had been waiting for me to reach a decision, were delighted to learn I would be returning and eagerly started readying their travel packs for the journey.

Three or four laymen, men with whom I had formed a close comradeship in the long months we had been practicing together, came to see us off. They were accompanied by Shōju Rōshi himself. They walked along with us for a couple of leagues until we reached the foothills of the high mountains. There the trail began to climb, growing steep and rugged, making it impossible for the old Rōshi to go any farther.

We exchanged words of encouragement and were about to part when the master grasped my hand in his and, speaking in a low voice, said affectionately to me, "If you continue your practice and go on to produce men like yourself, you will repay in full measure the profound debt you owe the Buddhas and patriarchs. Although you leave here and go to take care of your sick master, you must not cease your efforts and be content with a small attainment. You must now focus assiduously on your post-satori training. Cast aside all and any connection with the dust of the world, however slight it may appear. Vow never to give it the least concern. If you have the opportunity, come back and visit my small hermitage again someday."

He had finished speaking and was gone, but I was still bowed in reverence, my forehead pressed to the earth. As I began to ascend the winding mountain path that took me farther from him, my eyes were filled with tears.

EPILOGUE

This brings me to the close of the first chapter. There is still more to come, however. Another batch of verses left to be written. I 'm just going to dash off the words as they come into my head and not even give them a second look.

In the winter, the thirteenth of the twelfth month (the day of the year-end housecleaning), the second year of Meiwa [1765],[81] I was led by circumstances to compose this long string of clumsy verse. I now discover that I have three full chapters of the stuff. I started writing on the thirteenth of the twelfth month. I laid down my brush on the twenty-fifth, during the busy period just before the year's end. In that short span of thirteen days, I scribbled down all these idle words. The first book runs to seventy-two pages of manuscript, the second to sixty-one, and the last, I see, comes to fifty pages. A sum total of 179 sheets of paper; more than 2,500 verses; 18,000 Chinese characters. Not one word or phrase of it rises above the feeble and shoddy. Bad as it is, it is nonetheless a Dharma offering that originates in the Mind of Enlightenment. It's said even a superior man will make one mistake if he uses a thousand words, and even an inferior man may say one good thing if he uses a thousand words.[82] Here I am with 18,000 words! In all that (alas!), will there be even one good thing?

I feel ashamed of myself. Here I am, eighty-one years old, with a mind that has forgotten every word it ever knew. There are two young monks who attend me. Before I put brush to paper, I have to ask them how to write each character. If there is anything wrong with the way I have written them, the finger of disgrace must be pointed at them. This old monk accepts not one shred of the blame himself.

I only regret that in this inferior latter day, when the Dharma is fast declining, men of true understanding are so rare. You can scour the entire world without coming up with a single one. Nothing but blockheads wherever you go, men who couldn't tell the difference between a stone and a precious jade. I know what people of that ilk will say when they set eyes on this: "*Phuh! It's not even worth bending over to pick it up.*"

I have for all these many pages held up the uglinesses of my house for others to see, although not a single word of it could possibly do anyone a bit of good. You could smear the manuscript with sweet soft rice and leave it out under the trees for a thousand days: not even a crow would give it a second look. He would dismiss it out of hand. Revile it as filthy verbal refuse, break it up with his beak, scatter the pages over the ground, give them a last contemptuous spit, and fly off.

Still, I will not be resentful if people take no interest in it. If there is even a single superior seeker, one who has broken through the barrier, and he chances to glance at these lines, he will feel like someone who has encountered an old friend in a far-off land. I humbly and respectfully pass this work along to that patrician of the secret depths. May you penetrate the endless thickets of the thorn and briar forest!

I finished writing out this fair copy of the first volume on the fifteenth day of the first month, in the third year of Meiwa [1766].

Mu (Tōrei)

2
Post-satori Practice

ZEN SICKNESS

Plenty of greens in my kitchen, but the chopping blade won't cut;
Stoking the temple stove with autumn leaves, the fire tongs are busy.[1]

A FTER WE took our leave from Shōju, my companions and I pressed on and for several days, traversing difficult stretches of rugged terrain where the trail wound along towering mountain cliffs. After a long, arduous journey, we at last crossed into our home province. I went straight to Nyoka Rōshi's bedside and began ministering to his needs. Even as I nursed him, I complied faithfully with the injunction Shōju had given me when we parted at the foot of the mountains. Never for a moment was I remiss. Regularly and without fail, I sat for eight incense sticks of zazen each night.[2]

While crossing over the mountainous country of Echigo and Shinano Provinces on the trip back, and on into southern Suruga, I experienced satoris both great and small, in numbers I could not even count. Unfortunately, shortly after that the heart fire, unbeknownst to me, began to rush upward, oppressing my lungs and parching them of their essential fluids. Before I knew it, I had developed an incurable disorder of the heart.

I began moping around in a dark, melancholy state. I was always nervous and afraid, weak and timid in mind and body. The skin under my arms was constantly wet with perspiration. I found it impossible to concentrate on what I was doing. I sought out dark places where I could go to be alone and just sat there motionless like a dead man. Neither acupuncture, moxacautery, nor medical potions brought me any relief.[3]

I was ashamed to return and show my face at Shōju's in my present state. I wanted to comb the country and search for a wise teacher who might be able to offer some cure for my condition. But I couldn't leave the master's sickbed, even for a short time. I tried praying to the gods and Buddhas, but that didn't do any good either.

As I was cudgeling my brain trying to come up with a way out of my predicament, a wonderful thing happened. A younger brother of mine—a monk named Hatsu (he later became Setten Oshō and resided at the Ryōun-ji)—happened to hear about Nyoka Rōshi's illness.[4] He made the long trip all the way from the Kantō district and asked to take over the task of caring for the master.

Overjoyed at this unexpected turn of fortune, I received the master's consent to leave, then quietly gathered my belongings into a travel pack and left the temple. My destination was the town of Yamada in Ise Province. My pretext for going was a lecture-meeting on the *Record of Hsi-keng* to be given by Jōsan Oshō.[5]

Traveling with *Spurring Students through the Zen Barrier* as my constant companion, I stopped off several times to visit noted Zen teachers along the way. I told them of the trouble I was having and asked them for assistance, but they all said the same thing: I was suffering from "Zen sickness," and there was nothing they could do for me. The last stop I made was to see old Egoku Oshō in Izumi Province.[6]

"Attempting to cure Zen sickness," he told me, "only makes it worse. Find the quietest, most secluded spot you can. Settle down there [and do zazen] with the intention of withering away together with the mountain plants and trees. You mustn't spend the rest of your life running all over the country looking for someone to help you."

Post-satori Pilgrimage

Despite Egoku's advice, because I wanted to be close enough to have occasional interviews with him, I made for the Inryō-ji, a Sōtō temple in nearby Shinoda, and put up for a while in their Zen Hall.[7]

There were at that time more than fifty men in residence in the hall. The seat next to mine was occupied by a monk named Jukaku Jōza. Jukaku was a superior monk who had a genuine aspiration for the Way. We found our minds to be in complete agreement. I felt as though we had known each other for many years.

On one occasion, the two of us engaged in a private practice session. We pledged to continue it for seven days and nights. No sleep. No lying down. We cut a three-foot section of bamboo and fashioned it into a makeshift *shippei*. We sat facing each other with the *shippei* placed on the ground between us. We agreed that if one of us saw the other's eyelids drop, even for a split second, he would grab the staff and crack him with it between the eyes.

For seven days, we sat ramrod-straight, teeth clenched tightly in total silence. Not so much as an eyelash quivered. Right through to the end of the seventh night, neither one of us had occasion to reach for that cudgel.

One night, a heavy snowfall blanketed the area. The dull,

muffled thud of snow falling from the branches of the trees created a sense of extraordinary stillness and purity. I made an attempt at a poem to describe the joy I felt:

> *If only you could hear*
> *the sound of snow*
> *falling late at night*
> *from the trees*
> *of the old temple*
> *in Shinoda!*[8]

About that time, the abbot of the Inryō-ji took me aside and told me that he wished to have me stay on at the temple as his successor. The temple holdings included some very rich and productive fields, making it possible to provide for forty or even fifty visiting monks at annual summer retreats.[9] Uppermost in my mind at the time was a trip to Hyūga in Kyushu to visit Kogetsu Rōshi,[10] so I found it difficult to come to a final decision. Shortly after, I obtained permission to leave the temple and struck out on my own for Kyoto. Jukaku slipped away from the assembly, walked along at my side for several leagues, and then turned back.

I was soon overtaken by a violent rainstorm. The water poured in sheets, turning the road to thick mud, which sucked at my ankles as I walked. But I pushed forward into the mist and pelting rain oblivious to it all, humming as I went.

All at once, I found I had penetrated a verse that I had been working on, Master Ta-hui's "Lotus leaves, perfect discs, rounder than mirrors; Water chestnuts, needle spikes, sharper than gimlets."[11] It was like suddenly seeing a bright sun blazing out in the dead of night. Overcome with joy, I tripped, stumbled, and plunged headlong into the mud. My robe was soaked through, but my only reflection was, "What's a muddy robe, compared to

51

the extraordinary joy I now feel?" I rolled over onto my back and lay there motionless, submerged in the mire.

Some other travelers happening by rushed up and stared with amazement and alarm at the figure lying dead in the mud. Hands grabbed at me and propped me up. "Is he unconscious?" they cried. "Is he dead?" someone asked.

When I returned to my senses, I began clapping my hands together with delight and emitting great whoops of laughter. My rescuers started backing away from me with doubtful grins on their faces. Then they broke and ran, yelling "Crazy monk! Crazy monk!" (It was a repeat performance of the events that had taken place some years before in Iiyama.) I had just experienced one of those eighteen satoris I mentioned before.[12]

I resumed my journey, stepping buoyantly down the road with a blissful smile on my face. I was plastered with mud from head to foot but so happy I found myself laughing and weeping at the same time. Although in no hurry to reach my destination, before I knew it, I was walking the streets of the capital.

"Those who meet will part; those who part will meet again"—true to that familiar rule of human life, I now ran into three or four old comrades just returned from a visit to Kogetsu's temple in Hyūga. We joined hands in joyful greeting. When I asked them how they had found Hyūga, they were unanimous in their endorsement of the master.

"Kogetsu is the kind of teacher who appears in the world once every five hundred years," they exclaimed. "He's like the Udumbara flower, which only blossoms every three thousand years. It's especially regrettable that you haven't been to see him yet, elder brother."[13]

Another monk who happened to be sitting nearby broke in to say, "Well, I don't know much about Udumbara flowers, but there's an old priest in Wakasa Province named Tetsudō.[14] He lives at the Enshō-ji near Obama and was an attendant for many years to Sekiin Rōshi, who was a direct Dharma heir of National Master Gudō. Tetsudō is a great priest: his strong, unwavering devotion to the Way is unequaled. People from all ranks and walks of life come from far and near to pay homage to him. The trust they place in him, their veneration for him, is great indeed."

By the time he was finished speaking, my excitement had risen to a considerable pitch. There was no doubt about it. Tetsudō, the priest he described, was a Dharma uncle of Shōju Rōshi in Iiyama! Any plans I had to go to other parts would have to be put aside for the time being.

Not knowing whether the Dharma path be far or near, my mind now moved along the narrow byways to Wakasa. The heart of man, like a black valley, can with polishing turn into a pure white stream. So, as helpless and forlorn as a frail bamboo-leaf boat, floating, sinking, I drifted yearningly on and on until at last I reached Obama's narrow shores.[15]

The Enshō-ji was not located where I thought it was, so I was obliged to continue on, asking directions as I went, until finally I stood before the gates of the old temple in the hamlet of Ozaki. Following an interview with Tetsudō Rōjin, I hung my traveling staff up to stay. During the short time I was there, I served as Tetsudō's attendant.

As I continued to mull over the counsel Egoku Rōshi had given me about seeking a secluded spot where I could devote myself quietly to practice, I happened to remember a grass hut located deep in the mountainous country near Sugeya in Mino Province. When the summer retreat ended, I obtained Tetsudō's permission to leave, strapped on my travel pack, and set out for Mino.

Once again with troubled steps I walked the roads of Ōmi. Possessing not a ray of hope, swallowing back some bitter tears, I entered Mino Province, then skulked my way to Sugeya, deep in the mountains of Horado.

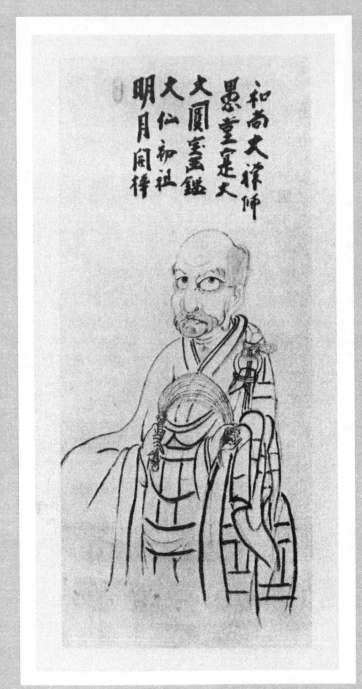

National
Master
Gudō

Being unsure of the exact location of the hermitage, I inquired around, only to discover, to my deep disappointment, that after the death of the old monk who had resided there, the building had fallen into decay. Nothing remained now, only a field of waving grain.

Now I was really at a loss, not knowing what to do or where to turn. Ultimately, I decided to go and take up residence in the Monks Hall of the Reishō-in in Iwasaki. There was a large contingent of more than fifty monks in training at the time. Sad to say, however, they were all pursuing the dry and lifeless methods of the "Unborn Zen" that had taken such a hold on people's minds in recent times. Aside from their morning and midday meals, on which they all did an admirable job, both old monks and young monks alike spent their days seated like lumps in long, lifeless ranks, nodding away like oarsmen. At night, they waited with pricked ears, listening for the bell to announce the end of the sitting period. Then they lined up their pillows in long rows and laid themselves down to sleep. As they did this, they chanted loudly back and forth, "Great happiness and peace. Great happiness and peace."[16]

I alone roused a dauntless spirit of great resolve, swearing I would not lie down even to rest. Never once did I allow myself to doze off. I can see now, looking back, that those nightly choruses of "Great happiness and peace" worked to excellent advantage by increasing my determination to forgo all sleep or rest.

Once, I overheard a small group of monks discussing me in hushed voices: "It's a shame about him. The great ignorant oaf. He's still doesn't know the first thing about the great vehicle and the secret of great happiness and peace to be found in the Unborn. That's why he always looks so worried and distressed. You can't help feeling sorry for him."

One day, when I was in the abbot's chambers, I brought the matter up with him: "I've observed how the men in the Monks

Hall all seem to make sleep and 'withered tree' sitting their most urgent concern. Surely they are headed for an extremely dismal rebirth when they die—the Black-Rope Hell or the Mountain-Crusher Hell. When that happens, don't you think they will resent you bitterly?"[17]

He told me this was all "unwanted meddling" on my part: poking into others' affairs would distract me from my own practice, and I should stop it.

"Master, was your own eye opened by doing what they are doing?" I asked.

"You shouldn't concern yourself with my eye either," he said.

"But you are an example for me, a model to observe and follow," I replied. "How can I do that unless I concern myself with your eye?"

"In the past," he said, "I used to believe the time would come when there would be a great breakthrough. I endured a great deal, lots of difficult practice, trying to achieve it."

"Then why," I replied, "don't you accept that your pupils might also achieve such a breakthrough at some point and make them endure austerities that can open up their eyes? If you leave them to their own devices, allow them to go on as they are, it is clear they will never open their eyes as long as they live. If they die in that state, they will certainly fall into the Black-Rope Hell. They will most assuredly resent you then."

"You should be concentrating on your own eye. That's all you need worry about," he said. "Forget about other people's eyes."

"My eye?" I replied. "As for that, you could take a hundred stone-breaking mallets, sledge and bludgeon day and night, without ever laying them down, but you still couldn't scratch its outer surface."[18]

The master gave a faint smile and abandoned the discussion.

National Master Musō's Solitary Retreat

There was another old priest living in those parts who went by the name of Tarumaru Sokai.[19] Another half-baked, muddle-headed member of the Unborn tribe. One day, he dropped by the temple and gave the following Dharma talk to the brotherhood:

> Years ago, the National Master Musō decided to spend the summer retreat alone in a mountain hut to devote himself to a practice regimen of rigorous austerity.[20] He climbed the slopes of Mount Kentoku in the province of Kai, empty-handed except for a single skewer of dried persimmons, and took up residence in the tiny hut. He pledged firmly that, instead of the two normal meals each day, he would eat nothing but a single dried persimmon.
>
> A young monk about fourteen or fifteen years of age, suddenly appeared out of nowhere, addressed Musō, and asked to be permitted to stay at the hut and serve as Musō's attendant during the summer retreat.
>
> "What an uncommon request to hear from a boy of your years in this day," Musō said admiringly. "But you don't know that I plan to live here on only one dried persimmon each day. I'm afraid there won't be anything for you to eat."
>
> "Share half of your persimmon with me, then," the boy said. Musō, taken somewhat aback, didn't know what to answer. As he was mulling a response, the boy continued: "I'll serve you all summer. On only half a dried persimmon a day. What is there for you to consider, master?"
>
> Musō reflected, "Even though he says that, he can't possibly stick out the whole summer on a few bits of dried persimmon. He'll be around a day or two, then he'll run off." With this in his mind, Musō told the boy he could stay.
>
> One month passed. Two months. Not only did the admirable young monk show no inclination to run off, he performed all his duties scrupulously, never slackening his efforts from first to last, whether he was engaged in his day-to-day chores or reading and

chanting sutras. Neither did he seem the least bit bothered by the lack of nourishment. He swept. He drew water. He worked hard and well.

On the morning of the final day of the retreat, Musō summoned the young monk. "You have done an excellent job," he told him. "The valuable support you have given me all summer long has helped immensely in allowing me to focus on my practice. I know this isn't much of a gift, but I want you to have it as a token of my appreciation for the service you have rendered this summer."

So saying, Musō lifted the surplice from around his shoulders and handed it to the boy. The boy accepted it, raising it up three times in veneration, and put it over his own shoulders.

"Master," he said, "as you leave this morning, you will come to a small hamlet at the foot of the mountain. To the left of the path you will see a house, recently rebuilt. The owner is a kinsman of mine. I'm going to hurry on ahead and ask him to have some food ready for your midday meal. You can take your time going down."

The boy made a parting bow, pressing his forehead to the earth, and sped off down the mountain path. He covered the ground almost as though he were flying.

Musō, aided by a bamboo staff, proceeded feebly, step by step, down the mountainside. It was nearly noon when he reached the hamlet. As he came to the newly built farmhouse the boy had described to him, a man emerged from the entrance. He hurried to where Musō stood, pressed his head to the ground in a deep bow, and said: "I'm very glad, and very relieved, to see you, master. I had expected you earlier and was just about to go up the mountain and start looking for you. Please, come into my house."

Musō asked where the young monk was.

"I was wondering that myself," the farmer replied. "He was here just a moment ago."

Stepping outside to see if he could catch sight of the boy, the farmer spotted one of his neighbors coming to the door.

"The strangest thing has just happened," said the man. "I saw a young monk—he couldn't have been more than thirteen or fourteen—fly straight through the latticework of the doors on that shrine over there. I couldn't believe my eyes. No human could have done that! I went over to the shrine and pushed apart some loose planks to look inside. There was no sign of one in there. I don't know what to make of it."

Musō's host listened in amazement. He went over to the shrine to have a look for himself. Opening the doors, he went inside and carefully searched the interior of the hall from wall to wall. Seeing nothing out of the ordinary, he was about to leave when something caught his eye. "How odd," he thought. "That three-foot statue of Jizō Bodhisattva standing serenely in the corner there is wearing the very same damask surplice I saw on that young monk just a few hours ago.[21] It's so eerie it frightens me."

In the meantime Musō, learning what had happened, rushed over to the shrine. He entered, took one look at the statue of Jizō, and immediately placed his palms together before him in homage. Then, overcome with tears, he dropped to the floor in a deep bow. Villagers who were clustering around the doorway began sobbing, too, and followed Musō's example by prostrating themselves in veneration, the scene impressed indelibly on their minds.

When Musō was finally able to suppress his tears, he exclaimed, "I cannot believe what has happened. My old surplice. I had worn it for years. I gave it to the young monk just this morning to reward him for his help during my retreat. Look at the Bodhisattva's face! And the rest of his appearance. The mirror image of that young monk! There is not the slightest difference.

"How unworthy I have been! I didn't have any idea he was Jizō Bodhisattva. But even so, I still didn't grant him so much as a bow. I made him work very hard all summer long. How frightening that I remained completely unaware of the Buddha's unknown working."

A great wave of excitement now spread through the village. "It was Jizō Bodhisattva!" villagers exclaimed in wonder and admiration. "The young monk we saw this summer up on the mountain following the master around was really this Jizō Bodhisattva."

People from places all over the district, some from as far as five leagues distant—young and old, men and women, priests and laity, all social ranks—began filing into the shrine. An unbroken stream of pilgrims that continued without cease for eight or nine days. All who came promptly expressed their respect and undying devotion for National Master Musō. It is a story that has been handed down from generation to generation on the lips of village elders far and wide.

As Tarumaru finished telling his story, the monks were all wringing the tears from their sleeves. "What a splendid story." "What a splendid story . . ." they mumbled over and over.

But I thought to myself: "What those village elders admired and revered, what all those pilgrims came to worship—that's not what I'm after. I value Musō's deep faith and steadfastness of purpose. I envy his pure, unswerving dedication to the Way. I want to do as he did, find a pure, consecrated spot, quiet and secluded, where no one ever comes. I don't think I'm quite up to a daily ration of a morsel or two of dried persimmon, but if I could get a fistful of rice to boil up into a daily bowl of gruel, I'd like to spend a summer finding out how strong my dedication to the Way really is."

SOLITARY RETREAT

I waited until the retreat ended, then privately asked the abbot for permission to leave. I struck out, with no particular destination in mind, headed in the general direction of Mount Kokei.[22] Wandering along, moaning audibly in my distress, through wild and desolate moorlands barren of all human habitation, I found the going especially hard with no companion at my side with whom I might converse. I reached the relay station at Ōta more troubled and miserable than ever.[23] In the distance off to the left of the road, I spotted just the kind of pure, unprofaned temple I was looking for. As it was well past noon, I decided to ask for some tea to have with my lunch. I bent my steps to the entrance of the temple, removed my sedge hat, and stepped inside.

"Please, may I have a cup of tea?" I called out.

The incumbent of the temple (the Manshaku-ji) who appeared to greet me turned out to be one Chin Shuso, a great friend of mine I hadn't seen for several years.[24] Meeting again so unexpectedly was a great surprise to us both. We grabbed hands, half laughing, half crying with delight. We spent the whole afternoon talking over old times and comparing our hopes for the future. I put up that night at the temple but told Chin I would have to leave for Mount Kokei the very next morning.

"Now that you've come here," he said, "what reason could you have for wanting to go on to Kokei?"

So I told him candidly what I had on my mind.

"Well," he said, "if you don't find the mountains at Kokei to your liking, be sure to come back. I think I may know of a place for you myself." The next morning we parted, our eyes moist with tears.

I trudged forlornly on, my mind set on "withering away together with the mountain trees and grasses," but with no idea where I might find a place suitable for such a purpose. Here again, old Shōju's lamentation about "looking for stars in the midday skies" came to mind.[25] With my heart sighing like the wind that whips the ocean into angry white waves and threshes through the pine forests, I continued down the untrodden roads. I soon discovered I had entered an area of great beauty. Its splendid mountain foliage and sanctity of setting could not have been equaled even by those landscapes celebrated in the classical poetry of China and Japan.

As I was hunting around and questioning people, trying to

find a place to stay, I ran into a former acquaintance who was now living as the master of a small mountain temple. We spent the next few days discoursing deeply and extensively about matters related to spiritual life.

Meantime, I looked high and low, I asked all around, but in the end, I failed to find any place that suited me. I returned in fallen spirits to the Manshaku-ji.

I was greeted by Chin. "I knew you'd be back," he said. "The other day, I located the very place you've been looking for. It's an ideal sanctuary, completely cut off from the dust of the world—as quiet as samadhi. It's in the mountains about a league north of here, at a place called Iwataki.[26] It's being offered by an elderly gentleman named Shikano Tokugen. Layman Tokugen is very wealthy and is a devotee of the Pure Land teaching. I've already taken the liberty of telling him about you and your career. He agreed immediately to have a small hermitage built for you to reside in. While it's being constructed, you can go and seclude yourself at a place called Kawaura. It's not far from here. As soon as the hermitage is ready, I'll come and get you myself."

After I was a little over a month in Kawaura, Chin showed up and escorted me to Tokugen's residence. I moved into the new hermitage, Iwataki-an, the very next day.

The old layman instructed Shikano Kanji, his eldest son and heir, to show me the way up to the hermitage. A servant followed along behind us carrying a plain wooden bucket, the kind that contains a five-bushel load of rice. It wasn't long, only a league or so, before we arrived at the hermitage.

Once inside, I offered a stick of incense, performed three bows, assumed a zazen posture, and sat there silent and motionless. Kanji pressed his palms together and bowed to me. Then he set off back down the mountain, and I was all alone.

3

Mount Iwataki

REFLECTIONS ON DO-NOTHING ZEN

ALONE IN the hut, I thrust my spine up stiff and straight and sat right through until dawn. All through the night, the room was haunted by a terrifying demonic presence. Since I dislike having to swell the narrative with such details, however, I won't describe it here.[1]

In the morning, I opened the rice pail, reached inside with my left hand, and grasped a fistful of the grains. I boiled these up into a bowl of gruel, which I ate in place of the two regular meals. I repeated the same routine each day. I wonder, was my regimen less demanding than National Master Musō's, with his half persimmon?[2]

After a month of this life, I still hadn't experienced a single pang of hunger. On the contrary, my body and mind were both fired with a great surge of spirit and resolve. My nights were zazen. My days were sutra-recitation. I never let up. During this period, I experienced small satoris and large satoris in numbers beyond count. How many times did I jump up and jubilantly dance around, oblivious of all else! I no longer had any doubts at all about Ta-hui's talk of eighteen great satoris and countless small ones. How grievously sad that people today have discarded this way of kenshō as if it were dirt!

Akiba Gongen

As for sitting, sitting is something that should include fits of ecstatic laughter—brayings that make you slump to the ground clutching your belly. And when you struggle to your feet after the first spasm passes, it should send you kneeling to earth in yet further contortions of joy.[3]

But for the past hundred years, ever since the passing of National Master Gudō,[4] advocates of blind, withered-up, silent illumination Zen have appeared within the Rinzai, Sōtō, and Ōbaku schools. In spots all over the country, they band together, flicking their fingers contemptuously, pishing and pughing: "Great satori eighteen times! Small satoris beyond count! Pah! It's ridiculous. If you're enlightened, you're enlightened. If you're not, you're not. For a human being, the severing of the life-root that frees you from the clutches of birth-and-death is the single great matter. How can you count the number of times it happens—as if it were a case of diarrhea!

"Ta-hui made statements like that because he was ignorant of the supreme, sublime Zen that is to be found at the highest reaches of attainment. Supreme Zen, at the highest reaches, does not belong to a dimension that human understanding of any kind can grasp or perceive. It is a matter of simply being Buddhas the way we are right now—'covered bowls of plain unvarnished wood.' It is the state of great happiness and peace, the great liberation.[5] Put a stop to all the chasing and hankering in your mind. Do not interfere or poke around after anything whatever. That mind-free state detached from all thought is the complete and ultimate attainment."

These people, true to their words, do not do a single thing. They engage in no act of religious practice; they don't develop a shred of wisdom. They just waste their lives dozing idly away like comatose badgers, useless to their contemporaries while they live, completely forgotten after they die. They aren't capable of leaving behind even a syllable of their own to repay the profound debt they owe to the Buddha patriarchs.

Maintaining come hell or high water, "We are Buddhas just as we are—plain unvarnished bowls," they proceed to consume heaping piles of rice day after day. They then disburden themselves of steaming loads of horse flop—great copious pillows of the stuff! That is the sum total of their achievements. They can't help a single person to the other shore of emancipation so as to repay the obligation they owe to their own parents. To them, the Buddhist saying "If one child leaves home for the priesthood, his kinsmen will be born in the heavenly realms for nine generations" is just so much hogwash.

To them, I say: "Surely you must know there are fifty-two stages of practice a Bodhisattva passes through in becoming a Buddha, beginning with the arising of the religious mind and ending with the final stages of supreme enlightenment. For some Bodhisattvas, enlightenment comes suddenly, and for some, it is gradual. For some, attainment is complete, and for others, it is partial. If you are right about 'being as you are' in this 'plain bowl' suchness of yours, then the stages of Bodhisattva practice that were set forth long ago are mistaken. If the stages passed down from the past are correct, then being as you are, like a 'plain bowl,' is wrong. The Buddha once told his disciples he would rather they be reborn as cankered old foxes than to see them become followers of the Two Vehicles.[6] But followers of the Two Vehicles are nothing compared to you, you ignorant, shameless, unconscionable, self-indulgent pack of scoundrels!"

Take the case of the man called Sanuki. During his lifetime, he was a disciple of the priest Ronshikibō of Ikoma. Not long ago, his tormented spirit took possession of his younger sister in Tōtōmi Province. He described to her the terrible agony he was suffering in hell and begged her to help him.[7]

Another man, a learned priest, because of the karmic obstacles he had created for himself by spreading the teachings of Unborn Zen, became a wild fox spirit and took possession of the head priest of one of our large and important Shinto shrines.

After Shōgetsu Shōnin died, he turned into a fine, sleek horse. Then he became a turtle. He can be seen paddling in the Nagara River.

An old woman, a resident of Kyoto, died not long ago. In her youth, she had followed the Pure Land teachings; her devotion to the Nembutsu was second to none. But in her middle years, she took to believing the false teaching of the Unborn, a doctrine that holds that death is the end of all existence.[8] Before she knew it, she was using a false measure to cheat her customers. In doing this, she accumulated a great deal of bad karma that caused her to fall into one of the terrible realms of hell when she died. In Kyoto last summer, she took possession of the young daughter of a wealthy family. After explaining to the girl in great detail the painful retribution she was experiencing, she said, "I have nothing against you or your family. While I was alive, I recited Buddhist sutras. I worked earnestly, performing various good deeds, doing my best to avoid falling into hell. Then one day, I heard the teaching of a good and learned priest. 'You mustn't chant sutras,' he said. 'You mustn't do zazen. You are Buddhas just the way you are now. Once you're dead and your remains are consumed in the flames, what future life can there be then?' It is my great sorrow and misfortune that, after I heard him speak, I ceased all the good deeds and practices I had until that very moment been so earnestly engaged in. How could I have known I would sink to cheating people with a false measure and wind up in hell?

"I began looking around for someone who could help me escape from the horrible fate that has befallen me. None of my own friends or relations seemed suitable, so I was obliged to seek elsewhere. I happened to see the luxurious residence where you dwell with your wealthy family. Although I had no feelings one way or the other toward you or the other members of your family, I decided to take possession of you—the precious young daughter—and appeal to you for help.

"Seek out a priest of unsurpassed learning. Make offerings to the Buddhas. Conduct maigre feasts for the priests. Do whatever you have to, but please save me from this endless agony!"

A lecture-meeting was being held at the Tōfuku-ji in Kyoto; Daikyū Oshō was delivering a series of talks on the *Record of Wu-chun*.[9] The young girl went to the Tōfuku-ji, told Daikyū her story, and begged him to lend his assistance. Daikyū, after conferring with the assembled priests, decided to conduct a *Suiriku* ceremony.[10] Daikyū himself presided, offering incense and reading out a religious verse he had composed for the release of the tormented soul. Soon afterward, the spirit revealed that it had attained immediate release and had gone on to a joyous rebirth in the heavenly realms.

See what an immense difference separates the true from the false. The true Dharma and false Dharmas as well—both are greatly to be feared, and we must be extremely careful not to mistake one for the other. One priest, by preaching a false Dharma and telling people to sit lifelessly in the Unborn, instilled in them the false notion that everything ends with death. He was thus directly responsible for sending a devout laywoman straight to rebirth in the terrible realms of hell. Another priest, on the strength of but a few lines of verse, was able to free the woman instantly from the incessant agony of the scorching hells. The true and the false are more distant from each other than heaven is from earth.

ADVICE FROM A STUDENT

An elderly gentleman once took the occasion of a personal interview [*dokusan*] to offer me a piece of advice. After reverently performing his bows, he declared with great solemnity: "It's said that when speaking out will do no good, it is better to remain silent. I believe what I have to say will do some good, yet like many medicines effective for curing illnesses, you may find it bitter and difficult to take. Honest words of advice may sound harsh when one hears them yet still be of value in changing one's behavior.

"Master, I have been wanting to give you this advice for a long time now, but I have kept my counsel, fearing it would strike you the wrong way. Deep in my heart, I wondered whether I was being disloyal in not speaking out."

"If I were ill," I said, "would you refrain from using medicine that could cure me because it had a bitter taste?"

The old man was delighted at my response and proceeded to tell me the following: "You have always detested the one-sided, sterile, lifeless sitting practices espoused by the teachers of Unborn Zen. You have abused them as if they were mangy curs covered with running sores. You have reviled them as if they were clods of matted filth. But if you continue your attacks on those unpriestly bands of silent illumination bonzes, they will come to regard you as their bitter enemy. Before long, they are sure to trump up perverse and unwarranted criticisms to level against you, to hatch clever plots of various kinds and use them to damage your good name as a virtuous priest. If that happens, what a great loss it will be for the Buddha Dharma.[11]

"Please give this warning due consideration, master. Leave those shriveled-up gangs of false Unborn Zennists alone. Don't bother with the quietist dimwits. Don't give them a thought. Why do I say this?

> *"The long-abandoned,*
> *long-lost Dharma trail*
> *a rush-choked field*
> *trod open again*
> *by this old man.*

"Master Gudō wrote this verse about himself. He inscribed it over one of his portraits.[12] But master, I believe you must write the same about yourself:

> "The long-abandoned,
> long-lost Dharma trail
> a rush-choked field
> trod open once again
> by this old man.

"For truthfully, a mere hundred years after Gudō's passing, the authentic spirit and traditions of our school had died out so completely that not a sound or smell remained of them. Then, thirty or forty years ago, they were revived again. You and you alone are responsible for that. What you have accomplished compares with the feats heroes such as Chang Liang and Ch'en P'ing achieved for the Chinese people.[13] Had either of those two men been sidetracked by some misfortune, the very country would have been imperiled; it might even have ceased to exist.

"So, too, with the Dharma. Were some misfortune to befall you, the wind of the true Zen spirit and tradition would fall to earth again. False Dharmas would rise up and take over as before. The Buddha's Dharma would sink and vanish into the dust.

"At such a time, how could I or anyone who regards himself as a child of the Buddhas just sit by and gaze upon the ruin and desolation! It is for this reason I have spoken out in this reckless manner, without stopping to consider the grave risk I was running.

"Please, master," he said, pressing his forehead to the floor, "consider my reasons for speaking out. Overlook my impudence."

"Excellent! Excellent!" I told him. "You are indeed a devoted retainer. One of the 'genuinely dutiful and unswervingly loyal.' How could I find fault with the words of such a man? Don't

"The long-abandoned,
long-lost Dharma trail
a rush-choked field
trod open again
by this old man."

worry, I speak out as I do for a reason. But even if some misfortune should befall me, everything I've ever done is for the sake of the Dharma. How can I begrudge it anything? Especially now. I'm an old man, more than eighty years old; the end could come at any second. The time I have left isn't worth considering. What are a few days one way or the other? Besides, even supposing I attained a span of eight hundred years like P'eng Tsu,[14] it still couldn't begin to compare with the First Principle that's been handed down to us through thirty-four generations of Zen patriarchs in India and China.

"It's like a single loyal and upright man gladly sacrificing all he owns and life and limb together for the sake of his native land. I speak out for a good reason, and even if I am visited by trouble of some kind, in order to repay the long-standing debt of gratitude I owe the Buddha-patriarchs, I will continue to place my trust in the benevolent god who stands guard over the Dharma. On that benevolent god, with utmost respect, I confer the name Wild Ivy deity.[15] So long as he remains firmly established in the world, even if the quietistic, withered-sitting methods of Unborn Zen were to spread and infest every corner of the land, the true wind would not sink into the dust."

This, moreover, is the substance of the Bodhisattva's vow, vast as the ocean, which I have solemnly pledged to carry out.

What is that "true wind" that has never once fallen to earth over the span of endless kalpas? It is the One Great Matter of human life: striving with fierce and courageous determination to bore through the barrier into kenshō.

A man of old has said that "the practice of Zen requires three essentials: a great root of faith, a feeling of great doubt, and a great, burning aspiration. Lack any one of these and you are like a three-legged cauldron with one leg broken off."[16]

The most important of the three is the great, burning aspiration. You may possess an abundance of deep-rooted faith and a great doubt as well, but if the burning aspiration is not present, the great and marvelous power for healing others will not develop, and you will be incapable of curing the besetting illnesses of mankind and liberating sentient beings. What are those besetting illnesses? Ignorance, the afflicting passions, birth-and-death—the very roots of karma.

What is a great, burning aspiration? The intense arousing of the mind in fearless determination to move forward to deliverance. So it is said, "attainment of Buddhahood comes in one instant of thought for sentient beings who are fearless and intrepid; for those who are indolent and slothful, the passage to Nirvana can take three long kalpas."[17]

Who are the indolent and slothful? The great and powerful enemy of all pilgrims who aspire to perfect themselves in the practice of the three vehicles. In short, it refers to the sleep demons of silent illumination Zen.

It was for reasons such as these that the Buddha himself long ago engaged in a considerable amount of "meddling" and "interference."[18] When his disciple Aniruddha was constantly succumbing to the sleep demon, the Buddha admonished him, "Conchs and clams and other shellfish doze off into naps of a thousand years, thereby losing the opportunity to encounter a Buddha when he appears in the world."

Aniruddha thereupon kindled a great, burning aspiration. He practiced diligently for seven days and seven nights without lying down for sleep or repose. All of a sudden, the great eye of wisdom blazed forth from within. It temporarily deprived him of the faculty of sight, but he had gained a reward greater even than being reborn as a man or god.[19]

Now if the Buddha's admonition was correct, the sleep-happy people today, sitting half dead on their cushions, are wrong. If the sleep-happy sitters of today are right, the Buddha's admonition was mistaken. Patricians of the secret depths! You should perform three bows and give the Buddha's words your careful scrutiny and deep contemplation. Strive diligently, all of you! Do not allow yourselves to be content with meager gains. If you climb a mountain, go all the way to the top! If you enter the ocean, explore it to its depths!

As you proceed, you will come up against some final difficult barriers: Su-shan's Memorial Tower, Nan-ch'uan's Death, A Thousand Snow-Capped Peaks, Yen-t'ou's Old Sail, The Water Buffalo Comes through the Window, Chao-chou's Dog Has No Buddha-Nature, The Triple Invalid, Two Kinds of Light, The Old Lady Burns the Hermitage, Chao-chou Sees Through the Old Woman, The Hemp Robe of Ching-chou, The Young Woman Leaves Samadhi, The Rhinoceros Fan, and Killing the Cat.[20]

These are known as the poison fangs and talons of the Dharma cave. They are also called divine life-usurping amulets. You must bore through them, one by one. After that, there is your post-satori practice. Whatever you do, never settle for paltry gains!

EXEMPLARS OF ZEN PRACTICE

Years ago, National Master Gudō, having completed his pilgrimage around the country, paid a visit to Yōzan Rōshi of the Shō-taku line of Myōshin-ji.[21]

During his dialogue with Yōzan, Gudō felt restricted and constrained. Yōzan reviled him angrily and pelted him with scolding shouts.

Furious at himself for his unexpected lack of freedom, Gudō stalked away into the mountains behind the temple. He found a large rock and sat down upon it to meditate, determined to sit through to the death. Swarms of mosquitoes gathered around

A monk [Hakuin] setting out on pilgrimage

him, distracting him and impeding him from pursuing his goal.
He stripped off his garments and, without a stitch on his body,
steadfastly resumed doing zazen. Mosquitoes from all parts of the
mountain now descended upon him in great black clouds. They
pierced his skin, they sucked his blood, subjecting him to untold
agony. But he just stretched his backbone straight as a ridgepole
and sat on with even greater determination. It was like one person
battling a host of ten thousand. Suddenly, without warning, he
died the Great Death, his body and mind falling completely away.
He had attained the great emancipation.

When dawn came and he opened his eyes, he saw that his
body was covered with mosquitoes: they were so thick, the color
of his skin could not be seen beneath them. He began slowly and
calmly to brush them off. They dropped to the ground and lay
around him like a thick carpet of crimson-red cherries.

Beside himself with joy, he began stamping his feet and
swinging his arms in a wild, involuntary dance. He returned to
Yōzan and gave him a detailed account of the realization he had
attained. Sharing with Gudō the intense joy of the moment, the
master gently patted him on the back and confirmed his attainment of the Buddha Dharma.

In later years, Gudō served as abbot at a number of temples,
including the Shōden-ji and Daisen-ji, and greatly stirred up the
true wind of the Zen school.[22] He was a solitary peak who tow-
ered abruptly above his contemporaries. Superior monks beyond
count—great and heroic men all—issued from his forge. There
was one in particular, an illustrious son who outshone even his
illustrious father. His name: Shidō Munan Anju.[23]

Munan produced three Dharma sons and heirs of his own:
Dōkyō Etan Rōkan of the Shōju-an hermitage in Iiyama, Shi-
nano Province; Tetsuzui Oshō of the Zenkai-ji in Matsuzaki, Izu
Province; and Chōmon Oshō of the Bodaiju-in in Sumpu.[24]

A virtuous man long ago said that "the arduous struggle un-

dergone by the worthies of the past has a radiance that will un-
questionably grow and prosper." Words of indisputable truth![25]
How could National Master Gudō have achieved the great and
glorious accomplishments he did if he had not run up against the
venomous teeth of those bloodthirsty insects? Or opened all those
countless temples and training halls? If the bitter struggle engaged in by those of the past is right, the withered-up do-nothing
sitters of today with their "silent illumination" and "great peace
and happiness" are dead wrong.

Take someone like my own teacher, Shōju Rōkan. There was
once a woodcutter living near Shōju's hermitage at Narasawa who
came upon a wolf cub while he was out working in the mountains.
He carried the cub home with him and fed it, and soon he became
deeply attached to the little animal. He set out into the forest one
day, followed by the now devoted young wolf, to cut down a large
tree. The wolf lay down nearby and waited as the woodcutter set
about his task. By a freak accident, the tree toppled suddenly in
an unexpected direction. The woodcutter looked on helplessly as
the main trunk of the tree landed directly on top of the wolf,
crushing him. Overwhelmed with grief and remorse, the woodcutter could do nothing but sadly dispose of the lifeless remains
and return home.

Beginning that very night, wolves from all corners of the
province began gathering around Iiyama. They ran wildly across
the countryside in packs large and small, their eyes glowing
fiercely with anger and resentment. Each night they descended
into the village. The streets were alive with wolves. They stole
into houses and dragged children four, five, six, even seven years
old outside, where the pack would set upon them and tear them
to pieces. The next morning remnants of the bodies would be
strewn about the streets. Their wolfish vengeance knew no
bounds. At first sign of darkness, the villagers would shut themselves inside their homes and bar their doors and windows fast.

Not a soul dared to venture outside. All movement in the village ceased.

Witnessing these events, Shōju recalled the life of self-negation the great teacher Shūhō Myōchō had led on the riverbanks near Shijō Bridge in Kyoto. "A good chance," he thought to himself, "to test the strength of my religious mettle."

He went to the village cemetery, where the wolves congregated in greatest numbers, fashioned a seat of grasses, and sat down upon it to meditate. He vowed to continue sitting for the next seven nights.

When darkness fell, wolves in numbers beyond count gathered at the cemetery where Shōju sat, their dark shapes padding around him on all sides. Suddenly, two or three swerved away from the pack and darted straight for him, hurtling over his head only at the last instant. Wolves began sniffing at his throat, butting and poking at his back. He could feel their warm snouts brazenly nuzzling up and down his legs and around the soles of his feet. Icy fear gripped his liver, his knees quaked like jelly, as the beasts probed and tested in a thousand different ways.

Shōju never once flinched or wavered through it all. He even sensed a secret joy upon feeling the courage and strength stir within him. He sat unharmed right through until the end of the seventh and final night. I heard this story from Shōju himself one evening when we were drinking tea together.

And how about the life of self-negation Myōchō Daishi practiced on the banks of the Kamo River?[26] Myōchō would test the strength of his religious purpose by repairing each night to the neighborhood of the Shijō Bridge and performing zazen, seated on a cushion of grasses. The capital was plagued at the time by gangs of young street ruffians. They would gather in groups of three and four, arguing the merits of the swords they carried. From there, they would proceed down to the river and run through the reeds, testing their swords by cutting down hapless beggars and outcasts they happened upon. Great numbers of such people fell victim to their blades.

One day, a band of these marauding hoodlums stole unperceived into the area near the Shijō Bridge and saw Myōchō meditating on his grass cushion. He seemed an ideal victim.

"I'll strike him first with the long sword," one of them called out. "Then you can take your turns."

The villains approached the seated figure, threatening him, their weapons poised to strike.

Yet Myōchō showed no indication of fear at all. He just kept sitting bolt upright, with a calm and blissful lack of concern.

One of the swordsmen paused, lowered his weapon, and stared long and hard at Myōchō. Suddenly, he pressed his palms together before him in an attitude of veneration.

"If we caused the death of this praiseworthy man of religion, it wouldn't do very much to demonstrate the sharpness of our blades," he said. "But we would be committing a horrendous sin." With that, they dropped their swords and fled. Myōchō has a poem about this period in his life:

> *Hardships still come*
> *one upon the other*
> *enabling me to see*
> *if my mind truly has*
> *cast off the world or not.*[27]

This is a story that should inspire students for a thousand years. The illustrious Daitoku-ji, which Myōchō later founded, the exceptional brilliance of his radiant virtue that has lasted throughout the years—it is all a consequence of the hard, merciless perseverance of his practice. If the extraordinary exertion put forth by those such as Myōchō Daishi in the past was correct, the "great peace and happiness" espoused by today's priests must be wrong.

The elder monks who trained under the tutelage of Master Gudō engaged repeatedly in weeklong sessions of zazen. They would not sleep or repose for seven days and seven nights. Tetsuzui Rōkan, during one of these practice periods, dozed off in spite of himself.[28] A venerable rat scurrying along a shelf nudged an old pot and sent it clattering to the floor. The noise woke Tetsuzui. He rose, turned to the rat, and performed three deep bows. "Well done! Well done! Thanks to your apt admonishment, I was able to drive the sleep demon away!"

Later, he began nodding again. This time, he was startled into instant wakefulness by the noise of a kitten chasing a baby rat. He got up and made three bows to the kitten. "Well done! Well done! Thanks to your admonishment, I have caught the sleep demon red-handed and made him my prisoner."

This is the reason why a priest like Tetsuzui Rōkan came to attain an understanding that was virtually unmatched in Suruga and the surrounding provinces.

Or take the case of Chōmon Rōshi.[29] He would often as he conversed about matters of the Way tell of his experiences as a young monk. He stubbornly refused to allow the sleep demons near him. Whenever they tried to approach, he would take some moxa and burn his flesh at the *sanri* and *kyokuchi* points.[30]

The extraordinary dedication shown by the ancients in their pursuit of the Way is something we should deeply respect and treasure. Not a single person in any temple or monastery today bears even a remote resemblance to them. I am deeply grieved to see the Zen groves in such a dire state of deterioration and ruin. Do you know who is to blame? The teaching of today's bogus priests is the cause of it all.

Someone said, "Master, a while ago you generously taught us about the three types of succession. I can't figure out which of those categories a priest such as yourself would belong to. Did you succeed your enemy, your benefactor, or a figure of authority?"[31]

"It's a long story," I said. "Briefly stated, I am one of the average, mediocre group. I succeeded my benefactor."

"Tell us about it," he said.

"Well, to confess the truth, my late master was one of those Zen teachers of recent times who espouse the blind, withered-up tenets of Unborn Zen. There wasn't a mundane thought in his head. He was completely ignorant of secular matters. It was always

> " 'Plain covered bowls
> of unfinished wood
>   straight from the hills—
> no lacquer to put on
> no color to wear off.' [32]

"He would tell us, 'We're all Buddhas just the way we are,' and would not allow himself to be concerned with anything, large or small. As a consequence of this, the old Shōin-ji fell into indescribable ruin. Impoverished and debt-ridden, it had leaky roofs. Damp, rotten floors."[33]

BACK AT SHŌIN-JI

While I was living there in the mountain hermitage at Iwataki, an elderly servant named Yake Shichibei,[34] who had served my beloved father, Layman Heishin Sōi, and his father and his father's father before that, came to Iwataki looking for me. In tracing me to the hermitage, he had made an arduous journey of more than a hundred leagues, through steep, mountainous terrain. After we had greeted each other, he told me: "Our old

Shōin-ji is destitute. Its roofs and walls are cracking and crumbling down. A few old worn-out tatami mats are all that's left on the floors: the straw coverings have disappeared. When it rains, you need a rain hat to move between the abbot's room and the monks' quarters.

"Your father was deeply distressed by this. He summoned me and said: 'Shichibei, did you know that my uncle Daizui Rōjin restored the old Shōin-ji many years ago?[35] Now, even as we speak, its walls crumble away. There is nothing remotely to match it anywhere in the country. Before long, the ruins will be plowed under. A patch of wild barley will be growing there. How can I sit idly by and watch that happen? There is only one person who can save the Shōin-ji now. My son Kaku Jōza. If he were to return and live there, I'm sure before long he would have the temple back the way it used to be in the old days.

"'I have no one else to turn to, Shichibei. I know travel isn't easy at your age, but you are the only person I can trust to go and find my son and persuade him to return to reside in Shōin-ji. If you do it, you will relieve me of a great burden and enable me to end my days with an easy mind.'

"And that," explained Shichibei, tears streaming down his cheeks, "is why I have come all this way to find you. I hope you will respect your father's wish and return home with me."

I remained silent for a moment, an old saying passing through my head: "Don't enter a state that is in danger. Don't remain in a state that is in turmoil."[36] If I gave up the pure, serene life I now enjoyed to put myself in a situation fraught with turmoil and trouble, I would be acting directly counter to the sage counsel of the ancients. Yet if I didn't go, I would disappoint my aging father's most deeply cherished hopes.

After some hard pondering, I decided to return to Hara, reside at Shōin-ji, and put up with its drastic poverty as long as my father was alive. I could always leave again later, after he passed away, and go where I pleased. So, putting the quiet of the hermitage behind me, I stopped by Tokugen Rōjin's residence at the foot of the mountain to say farewell, and then, with Shichibei at my side, I set out for home.

Once I was installed at Shōin-ji, I adopted a life at once simple and severe and did not give a thought to the poverty of the temple or the appalling emptiness of its storerooms. I fashioned a large basket out of green bamboo, climbed inside it, and did zazen. By combining the methods of Zen meditation with those of Introspective Meditation, I was able to practice them both at the same time. Thanks to the invaluable method of Introspective Meditation, I succeeded in dispelling all the troubles and indispositions that had plagued me so much in the past, and my health returned to normal.[37]

The perfect tranquillity and pure untrammeled life I now enjoyed surpassed by far anything I had experienced back in the days at Iwataki. Being unconcerned by the poverty at Shōin-ji and an utter stranger to wealth of any kind, it was as though I were living in a place isolated by a thousand leagues from all human habitation. The wealth of ten thousand daimyos could have added nothing to the happiness I felt. Nor did I now feel any need to seek rebirth in the human or heavenly realms.

Here at this post station on the eastern high road—an island floating amid the defilement of the world, surrounded by the hectic intercourse of rich and poor, the clamorous strife of right and wrong, the din and clatter of men and beasts constantly moving to and fro—who would have believed me if I had told them that life in such a setting was fully equal to the delicious solitude I had known among the cliffs and crags of Iwataki, far from the world's dust? And how but for the hardships I experienced during that time when I sustained myself on a daily handful of rice could I ever have known the tremendous joy that filled me now!

Years ago, Shōtō Rōkan of the city of Sendai was constantly

besieged by requests for specimens of his calligraphy. He always obliged petitioners by writing the same six characters: "Pleasure is the seed of suffering. Suffering is the seed of pleasure."[38] Those inscriptions in ink were treasures greatly to be cherished.

After long, hard reflection, I concluded that even if I continued to enjoy this life of quiet and solitude, unaware of the privation at the temple, and went on practicing the life-nurturing technique of Introspective Meditation, perhaps prolonging my life to a span of eight hundred years like P'eng Tsu, I would still be no different from a sleep-happy old polecat drowsing away down inside his comfortable old den.

IMPARTING THE DHARMA

I decided I would be far better off if I followed the parting advice Shōju had given me: to devote my energy to liberating the countless suffering beings of the world by imparting the great gift of the Dharma; to assemble a few select monks capable of passing through the barrier into genuine kenshō; to strive diligently toward creating conditions for the realization of a Buddha-land on earth and, in the process, carry into practice Bodhisattva vows.

When I resolved to embark on this grand and far-reaching program and send a handful of genuine monks out into the world, it was because I wanted to repay the immense debt I owed to the Buddhas and patriarchs.

Little by little, I worked out methods for imparting the Dharma gift. At first, I had only two or three monks here with me. Later, they were joined by others, like attracting like, until eventually their number swelled to more than a hundred and fifty. In recent years, we usually have three hundred monks in residence in and around the temple.

Through all those years, in response to circumstances, in

answer to requests, I have traveled extensively, visiting many different provinces, carrying out my mission of imparting the Dharma wherever I went. I don't remember all the temples, monasteries, and laymen's homes I have been to.

I've been to southern Izu four or five times. I've made the same number of trips up to southern Kai. I've traveled north all the way to Kiso and Hida. As far south as Bizen and Bitchū Provinces. I've been to Edo on at least four or five occasions. At meetings during those visits, I have given Zen lectures [*teishō*] on a great many texts: four or five times each on the *Lotus, Shurangama,* and *Vimalakirti Sutras;* six or seven times on the *Blue Cliff Record* and the *Record of Hsü-t'ang;* two or three times each on *Praise of the True School* and the *Three Teachings of the Buddha Patriarchs.* More times than I can remember on the *Kannon Sutra.* In addition, I have lectured on the *Record of Lin-chi; Ta-hui's Letters;* the *Records of Daitō, Fa-yen, Sung-yuan,* and *Bukkō;* the *Tsung-ying Verse Collection;* the *Poems of Cold Mountain; Spurring Students through the Zen Barrier;* the *Four-Part Collection; Ta-hui's Arsenal; Manjushri's Held-in-Hand Sutra; The Precious Mirror Samadhi; Dream Words from the Land of Dreams; Poison Stamens in a Thicket of Thorns;* the *Record of Daiō; The Song of the Mind-King;* and others so numerous I can't recall them all.[39]

There is an old saying: "When a superior man speaks a thousand words, he may make a single mistake. When an inferior man speaks a thousand words, he may achieve a single benefit." If within this rambling nonsense of mine a single benefit is indeed to be found, it might perhaps serve as a small Dharma gift.

My writing is gross-grained, the strokes of my brush a thick, vulgar chicken-scratch. Both of them are riddled with blunders of various kinds. Characters miswritten. One word mistaken for another. I just scribble it down on the paper, make them a "fair copy." They take it and carve it onto wooden blocks and print it off. Altogether I must have written twenty books that way. No matter. Any wise man who claps eyes on them is sure to fling them to the ground in disgust and spew them contemptuously with spit.

My literary labors: *Poison Stamens in a Thicket of Thorns; Lingering Light from Precious Mirror; Idle Talk on a Night Boat; My Teakettle; A Weed-Choked Field of Words; Goose Grass; Tea-Grinding Song; A Record of Four Filial Young Girls; A Childhood Tale; Yūkichi's Tale; Dream Words from the Land of Dreams; Tosen-shikō; An Application of Moxa; Snake Strawberries; The Record of Sendai's Comments on the Cold Mountain Poems; Horse Thistles; Dharma Talks Introductory to Lectures on the Record of Hsi-keng; Wild Ivy.* Only a rough list, but when you're as old and forgetful as I am, you can't be expected to remember everything.[40]

A layman spoke up: "What a great stroke of luck it is in this degenerate latter day to be blessed with the essentials of so true and genuine a Dharma. One can expect to encounter such favorable karmic fortune only once in many rebirths. I look forward with keen anticipation to hearing something more about Introspective Meditation."

"Fine," I told him. "I like to see students who are eager to ask questions. But when I do a lot of talking like this it always tires me out. Come back tomorrow and ask me again."[41]

The layman pressed his palms together, bowed deeply, and was gone.

4

Zen Sickness

L ONG AGO, Wu Ch'i-ch'u told Master Shih-t'ai:[1] "In order to refine the elixir, it is necessary to gather the vital energy.[2] To gather the vital energy, it is necessary to focus the mind. When the mind focuses in the ocean of vital energy or field of elixir located an inch below the navel, the vital energy gathers there. When the vital energy gathers in the elixir field, the elixir is produced. When the elixir is produced, the physical frame is strong and firm. When the physical frame is strong and firm, the spirit is full and replete. When the spirit is full and replete, long life is assured."

These are words of true wisdom.

The layman came again the next morning and repeated the request he had made the previous day.[3]

"Very well," I said, "I will explain to you the essentials of Introspective Meditation."

On the day I first committed myself to a life of Zen practice, I pledged to summon all the faith and courage at my command and dedicate myself with steadfast resolve to the pursuit of the Buddha Way. I embarked on a regimen of rigorous austerities, which I continued for several years, pushing myself relentlessly.

Then one night, everything suddenly fell away, and I crossed the threshold into enlightenment. All the doubts and uncertainties that had burdened me all those years suddenly vanished, roots

"In order
to refine the
elixir, it is
necessary
to gather
the vital
energy. . . ."

and all—just like melted ice. Deep-rooted karma that had bound me for endless kalpas to the cycle of birth-and-death vanished like foam on the water.

It's true, I thought to myself: the Way is not far from man.[4] Those stories about the ancient masters taking twenty or even thirty years to attain it—someone must have made them all up. For the next several months, I was waltzing on air, flagging my arms and stamping my feet in a kind of witless rapture.

Afterward, however, as I began reflecting upon my everyday behavior, I could see that the two aspects of my life—the active and the meditative—were totally out of balance. No matter what I was doing, I never felt free or completely at ease. I realized I would have to rekindle a fearless resolve and once again throw myself life and limb together into the Dharma struggle. With my teeth clenched tightly and eyes focused straight ahead, I began devoting myself single-mindedly to my practice, forsaking food and sleep altogether.

Before the month was out, my heart fire began to rise upward against the natural course, parching my lungs of their essential fluids.[5] My feet and legs were always ice-cold: they felt as though they were immersed in tubs of snow. There was a constant buzzing in my ears, as if I were walking beside a raging mountain torrent. I became abnormally weak and timid, shrinking and fearful in whatever I did. I felt totally drained, physically and mentally exhausted. Strange visions appeared to me during waking and sleeping hours alike. My armpits were always wet with perspiration. My eyes watered constantly. I traveled far and wide, visiting wise Zen teachers, seeking out noted physicians. But none of the remedies they offered brought me any relief.

MASTER HAKUYŪ

Then I happened to meet someone who told me about a hermit named Master Hakuyū, who lived inside a cave high in the mountains of the Shirakawa District of Kyoto. He was reputed to be three hundred and seventy years old. His cave dwelling was two or three leagues from any human habitation. He didn't like seeing people, and whenever someone approached, he would run off and hide. From the look of him, it was hard to tell whether he was a man of great wisdom or merely a fool, but the people in the surrounding villages venerated him as a sage. Rumor had it he had been the teacher of Ishikawa Jōzan[6] and that he was well versed in astrology and deeply learned in the medical arts as well. People who had approached him and requested his teaching in the proper manner, observing the proprieties, had on rare occasions been known to elicit a remark or two of enigmatic import from him. After leaving and giving the words deeper thought, the people would generally discover them to be very beneficial.

In the middle of the first month in the seventh year of the Hōei era [1710],[7] I shouldered my travel pack, slipped quietly out of the temple in eastern Mino where I was staying, and headed for Kyoto. On reaching the capital, I bent my steps northward, crossing over the hills at Black Valley [Kurodani] and making my way to the small hamlet at White River [Shirakawa]. I dropped my pack off at a teahouse and went to make inquiries about Master Hakuyū's cave. One of the villagers pointed his finger toward a thin thread of rushing water high above in the hills.

Using the sound of the water as my guide, I struck up into the mountains, hiking on until I came to the stream. I made my way along the bank for another league or so until the stream and the trail both petered out. There was not so much as a woodcutters' trail to indicate the way. At this point, I lost my bearings completely and was unable to proceed another step. Not knowing what else to do, I sat down on a nearby rock, closed my eyes, placed my palms before me in *gasshō*, and began chanting a sutra. Presently, as if by magic, I heard in the distance the faint sounds of someone chopping at a tree. After pushing my way deeper through the forest trees in the direction of the sound, I spotted a woodcutter. He directed my gaze far above to a distant site among the swirling clouds and mist at the crest of the mountains. I could just make out a small yellowish patch, not more than an inch square, appearing and disappearing in the eddying mountain vapors. He told me it was a rushwork blind that hung over the entrance to Master Hakuyū's cave. Hitching the bottom of my robe up into my sash, I began the final ascent to Hakuyū's dwelling. Clambering over jagged rocks, pushing through heavy vines and clinging underbrush, the snow and frost gnawed into my straw sandals, the damp clouds thrust against my robe. It was very hard going, and by the time I reached the spot where I had seen the blind, I was covered with a thick, oily sweat.

I now stood at the entrance to the cave. It commanded a prospect of unsurpassed beauty, completely above the vulgar dust of the world. My heart trembling with fear, my skin prickling with gooseflesh, I leaned against some rocks for a while and counted out several hundred breaths.

After shaking off the dirt and dust and straightening my robe to make myself presentable, I bowed down, hesitantly pushed the blind aside, and peered into the cave. I could make out the figure of Master Hakuyū in the darkness. He was sitting perfectly erect, his eyes shut. A wonderful head of black hair flecked with bits of white reached down over his knees. He had a fine, youthful complexion, ruddy in hue like a Chinese date. He was seated on a soft mat made of grasses and wore a large jacket of coarsely woven cloth. The interior of the cave was small, not more than five feet square, and, except for a small desk, there was no sign of household articles or other furnishings of any kind. On top of the desk, I could see three scrolls of writing—*The Doctrine of the Mean, Lao Tzu,* and the *Diamond Sutra.*[8]

I introduced myself as politely as I could, explained the

symptoms and causes of my illness in some detail, and appealed
to the master for his help.

CURE

After a while, Hakuyū opened his eyes and gave me a good hard
look. Then, speaking slowly and deliberately, he explained that
he was only a useless, worn-out old man—"more dead than alive."
He dwelled among these mountains living on such nuts and wild
mountain fruit as he could gather. He passed the nights together
with the mountain deer and other wild creatures. He professed to
be completely ignorant of anything else and said he was acutely
embarrassed that such an important Buddhist priest had made a
long trip expressly to see him.

But I persisted, begging repeatedly for his help. At last, he
reached out with an easy, almost offhand gesture and grasped my
hand. He proceeded to examine my five bodily organs, taking my
pulses at nine vital points. His fingernails, I noticed, were almost
an inch long.

Furrowing his brow, he said with a voice tinged with pity,
"Not much can be done. You have developed a serious illness. By
pushing yourself too hard, you forgot the cardinal rule of religious
training. You are suffering from meditation sickness, which is extremely difficult to cure by medical means. If you attempt to treat
it by using acupuncture, moxacautery, or medicines, you will find
they have no effect—not even if they were administered by a P'ien
Ch'iao, Ts'ang Kung, or Hua T'o.[9] You came to this grievous pass
as a result of meditation. You will never regain your health unless
you are able to master the techniques of Introspective Meditation.
Just as the old saying goes, 'When a person falls to the earth, it is
from the earth that he must raise himself up.' "[10]

"Please," I said, "teach me the secret technique of Introspective Meditation. I want to begin practicing it, and learn how it's done."

With a demeanor that was now solemn and majestic, Master Hakuyū softly and quietly replied, "Ah, you are determined to find an answer to your problem, aren't you, young man? All right, I suppose I can tell you a few things about Introspective Meditation that I learned many years ago. It is a secret method for sustaining life known to very few people. Practiced diligently, it is sure to yield remarkable results. It will enable you to look forward to a long life as well.[11]

"The Great Way is divided into the two instruments of yin and yang. Combining, they produce human beings and all other things. A primal inborn energy circulates silently through the body, moving along channels or conduits from one to another of the five great organs. Defensive energy and nutritive blood, which circulate together, ascend and descend throughout the body, making fifty complete circulations in each twenty-four-hour period.[12]

"The lungs, manifesting the metal principle, are a female organ located above the diaphragm. The liver, manifesting the wood principle, is a male organ located beneath the diaphragm. The heart, manifesting the fire principle, is the major yang organ; it is located in the upper body. The kidneys, manifesting the water principle, are the major yin organ; they are located in the lower body. Contained within the five internal organs are seven marvelous powers, with the spleen and kidneys having two each.[13]

"The exhaled breath issues from the heart and the lungs; the inhaled breath enters through the kidneys and liver. With each exhalation of breath, the defensive energy and nutritive blood move forward three inches in their conduits; they also advance three inches with each inhalation of breath. Every twenty-four hours, the defensive energy and nutritive blood make fifty complete circulations of the body.

93

"Fire is by nature light and unsteady and always wants to mount upward, whereas water is by nature heavy and settled and always wants to sink downward. If a person ignorant of this principle strives too hard in his meditative practices, the fire in his heart will rush violently upward, scorching his lungs and impairing their function.

"Since a mother-and-child relationship obtains between the lungs, representing the metal principle, and the kidneys, representing the water principle, when the lungs are afflicted and distressed, the kidneys are also weakened and debilitated. Debilitation of the lungs and kidneys saps and enfeebles the other organs and disrupts the proper balance within the six viscera.[14] This results in an imbalance in the function of the body's four constituent elements (earth, water, fire, wind), some of which grow too strong and some too weak. This leads, in turn, to a great variety of ailments and disorders in each of the four elements. Medicines have no effect in treating them. Physicians can only look on with folded arms."

SUSTAINING LIFE

[Master Hakuyū continued:] "Sustaining life is much like protecting a country. Whereas a wise lord and sage ruler always thinks of the common people under him, a foolish lord and mediocre ruler concerns himself exclusively with the pastimes of the upper classes. When a ruler becomes engrossed in his own selfish interests, his nine ministers vaunt their power and authority, the officials under them seek special favors, and none of them gives a thought to the poverty and suffering of the people below them. The countryside is filled with pale, gaunt faces; famine stalks the land, leaving the streets of the towns and cities littered with corpses. The wise and the good retreat into hiding, the common

Bodhidharma

people burn with resentment and anger, the provincial lords grow rebellious, and the enemies on the borders rise to the attack. The people are plunged into an agony of grief and suffering until, finally, the nation itself ceases to exist.

"On the other hand, when the ruler turns his attention below, focusing on the common people, his ministers and officials perform their duties simply and frugally, the hardships and suffering of the common people always in their thoughts. As a result, the farmers produce an abundance of food, their wives an abundance of cloth. The good and the wise gather to the ruler to render him service, the provincial lords are respectful and submissive, the common people prosper, and the country grows strong. Each person is obedient to his superior, no enemies threaten the borders, and the sounds of battle are no longer heard in the land. The names of the weapons of war themselves come to be forgotten.

"It is the same with the human body. The person who has arrived at attainment always keeps the heart's vital energy below, filling the lower body. When the lower body is filled with the heart's vital energy, there is nowhere within for the seven misfortunes to operate[15] and nowhere without for the four evils[16] to gain an entrance. The defensive energy and nutritive blood are replete, the heart and mind vigorous and healthy. The lips never know the bitterness of medical potions; the body never feels the discomfort of the acupuncture needle or moxa treatments.

"An average or mediocre person always allows the heart's vital energy to rise up unchecked so it diffuses throughout the upper body. When the heart's vital energy is allowed to rise unchecked, the heat emanating from the heart on the left side damages the lungs on the right. This puts a strain on the five senses, diminishing their working, and causes harmful disturbances in the six roots.[17]

"Because of this, Chuang Tzu said, 'The True Person

breathes from his heels. The ordinary person breathes from his throat.'

"Hsü Chun said, 'When the vital energy is in the lower heater, the breaths are long; when the vital energy is in the upper heater, the breaths are short.'[18]

"Master Shang Yang said,[19] 'There is a single genuine vital energy in man. Its descent into the lower heater signifies the return of the single yang. If a person wants to experience the occasion when the yin reaches completion and yields to returning yang, his proof will be found in the warmth that is generated when the vital energy is concentrated in the lower body.'

"The golden rule in the art of sustaining life is always to keep the upper body cool and the lower body warm.

"There are twelve conduits along which the defensive energy and nutritive blood circulate through the body.[20] These conduits correspond to the twelve horary signs or stems, to the twelve months of the year, and to the twelve hours of the day. They also correspond to the various permutations the hexagrams or divination signs in the *Book of Changes* undergo in the course of their yearly cycle.

"Five yin lines above and one yang line below—the hexagram known as 'Ground Thunder Returns'—corresponds seasonally to the winter solstice. It is perhaps this Chuang Tzu refers to when he speaks of 'the True Person breathing from his heels.'

"Three yang lines below and three yin lines above—the hexagram 'Earth and Heaven at Peace'—corresponds seasonally to the first month, when the ten thousand things are pregnant with the vital energy of generation and the myriad buds and flowers, receiving the beneficial moisture, burst into blossom. It is the configuration of the True Person, whose lower body is filled with primal energy. When a person achieves this stage, his defensive energy and nutritive blood are replenished and his spirit is full of vigor and courage.

"Five yin lines below and one yang line above—the hexagram known as 'Splitting Apart'—corresponds seasonally to the ninth month. When the heavens are at this point, foliage in the garden and forest drains of color, flowers droop and wither. It is the configuration of the 'ordinary man breathing from his throat.' When a person reaches this stage, he is thin and haggard in appearance; his teeth grow loose and fall.

"Because of this, the *Treatise on Prolonging Life* states:[21] 'When all six yang lines are exhausted and man is wholly yin, death may easily occur.' What you must know is that, for sustaining life, the key is to have primal energy constantly filling the lower body."

REMEDIES FOR SUSTAINING LIFE AND ACHIEVING IMMORTALITY

[Master Hakuyū continued:] "Before Wu Ch'i-ch'u visited Master Shih-t'ai long ago,[22] he prepared himself by performing ritual purifications. Then he went and inquired about the art of refining the elixir. Master Shih-t'ai told him, 'I possess a marvelous secret for producing the genuine and profound elixir, but only a person of superior capacity would be able to receive and transmit it.' This is the very same secret the Yellow Emperor was given by Master Kuang Ch'eng. The Yellow Emperor received it only after he had completed a retirement and abstinence of twenty-one days.[23]

"The genuine elixir does not exist apart from the Great Way; the Great Way does not exist apart from the genuine elixir. You Buddhists have a teaching known as the five nonleakages.[24] Once the six desires are dispelled and the working of the five senses is forgotten, the primal, undifferentiated energy will gather to repletion under your very eyes. This is what T'ai-pai Tao-jen meant when he spoke about 'combining one's vital inborn energy with the primal energy of heaven and earth whence it derives.'[25]

"You should draw what Mencius called the 'vast, expansive energy' down and store it in the elixir field—the reservoir of vital energy located below the navel.[26] Hold it there over the months and years, preserving it single-mindedly, sustaining it without wavering. One morning, you will suddenly overturn the elixir furnace, and then everywhere, within and without the entire universe, will become a single immense piece of pure elixir.[27]

"When that happens, you will realize for the first time that you yourself are a genuine sage, as unborn as heaven and earth, as undying as empty space. At that moment, your efforts to refine the elixir will attain fruition. This is not a superficial feat such as raising winds or riding mists, shrinking space, or walking over water, the kind of thing that can be performed by lesser sages. For you, the object is to churn the great sea into finest butter, to transform the great earth into purest gold.[28]

"In explaining the phrase 'the metal liquid returns to the elixir,' a wise man of the past said, ' "Elixir" refers to the elixir field, and "liquid" refers to the blood fluid in the lungs, so the phrase means that the blood in the lungs returns to the elixir field located below the navel.' "[29]

DRAWING THE MIND INTO THE LOWER BODY

At this point, I [Hakuin] said to Master Hakuyū: "I am deeply grateful for your instruction. I'm going to discontinue my Zen study for a while so that I can concentrate my efforts on Introspective Meditation and cure my illness.

"There is something that still bothers me, however. Wouldn't the method you teach be an example of 'overly emphasizing cooling remedies in order to bring the heart-fire down,' which the great physician Li Shih-ts'ai warned against?[30] And if I concentrated my mind in a single place, wouldn't that impede the movement of defensive energy and nutritive blood and make them stagnate?"

A flicker of a smile crossed Master Hakuyū's face. "Not at all," he replied. "You mustn't forget that Master Li also said the nature of fire is to flame upward, so it must be made to descend; the nature of water is to flow downward, so it must be made to rise. This condition of fire descending and water ascending is called intermingling. The time when intermingling is taking place is called Already Completed; the time when it is not taking place is called Before Completion.[31]

"Intermingling is a configuration of life. Not intermingling is a configuration of death. When Master Li and those of his school speak of 'overly emphasizing cooling remedies to bring down the heart-fire,' they do so in order to save people who study the teachings of the Tan-hsi school from the harm that could result from over-emphasizing such remedies.[32]

"Fire functions in two ways: as prince and as minister. The princely fire is found in the upper body; it presides in tranquillity. The ministerial fire is found in the lower body; it presides in activity. Princely fire is master of the heart. Ministerial fire works as its subordinate.

"Ministerial fire is of two kinds, one of which is found in the kidneys, the other in the liver. The kidneys correspond to the dragon, the liver to thunder. There is a saying: 'The crash of thunder is never heard as long as the dragon stays hidden in the depths of the sea. The dragon never soars in the skies as long as thunder remains confined to the marshes and bogs.' Assuming that is true, and in view of the fact that the composition of both seas and marshes is water, doesn't the saying signify that the ministerial fire's tendency to rise is suppressed?

"It is also said that the heart becomes exhausted [of energy] when it tires and thus overheats. When the heart is exhausted, it can be replenished by making it descend below and intermingle with the kidneys. This is known as replenishing. It corresponds to the principle of After Completion mentioned before.

"You, young man, developed this grave illness because the fire in your heart was allowed to rush upward against the natural flow. Unless you succeed in bringing your heart down into your lower body, you will never regain your health, not even if you master all the secret practices the three worlds have to offer.[33]

"You probably regard me as some kind of Taoist. You probably think what I've been telling you has no relation to Buddhism at all. But that's mistaken. What I'm teaching you is Zen. If, in the future, you get a glimpse of true awakening, you will smile as you recall these words of mine."

NONCONTEMPLATION

[Master Hakuyū continued:] "As for the practice of contemplation, true contemplation is noncontemplation. False contemplation is contemplation that is diverse and unfocused.[34] You contracted this grave illness by engaging in diverse contemplation. Don't you think that now you should save yourself by means of noncontemplation? If you take the heat in your heart, the fire in your mind, and draw it down into the region of the elixir field and the soles of the feet, you will feel naturally cool and refreshed. All discrimination will cease. Not the slightest conscious thought will occur to raise the waves of emotion. This is true meditation— pure and undefiled meditation.

"So don't talk about discontinuing your study of Zen. The Buddha himself taught that we should 'cure all kinds of illness by putting the heart down into the soles of the feet.' The Agama sutras teach a method in which butter is used. It is unexcelled for treating debilitation of the heart.[35]

"In the Tendai sect's *Great Concentration and Insight*, the fundamental causes of illness as well as the methods of treating them are set forth in minute detail.[36] Twelve breathing techniques are given that are effective in curing a wide range of ailments. There is another technique of visualizing the heart as a bean resting on the navel. Ultimately, the essence in all these methods is to bring the heart-fire down and gather it in the elixir field and the soles of the feet. It is not only effective for curing illness, it is extremely beneficial for Zen meditation as well.

"There are, I believe, two kinds of concentration: concentration on ultimate truth and concentration on temporary truth.[37] The former is a full and perfect meditation on the true aspect of all things; in the latter, primary importance is placed on focusing the heart-energy in the region of the elixir field. Students who practice these concentrations derive great benefit from them."

CULTIVATING THE MIND ENERGY

[Master Hakuyū continued:] "Dōgen, founding patriarch of the Eihei-ji temple, traveled to China and studied with Zen master Ju-ching at T'ien-t'ung monastery.[38] One day, when he went to Ju-ching's chambers to receive his instruction, Ju-ching said, 'When you practice zazen, you should place your mind in the palm of your left hand.'

"This generally corresponds to the Tendai sect's concentration on temporary truth.

"In his *Smaller Concentration and Insight*, Chih-i relates how he first came to teach the secret technique of Introspective Meditation (concentration on temporary truth) and how by using it he saved his elder brother, gravely ill, from the brink of death.[39]

102

"The priest Po-yün said, 'I always keep my heart down filling my lower belly. I use it all the time—teaching students, guiding the assembly of monks, receiving visitors, during encounters in my chambers, while busily engaged in talks and lectures of various kinds—and I never use it up. Since reaching old age, I've found its benefits to be especially great.'[40]

"How commendable! Don't Po-yün's words agree with the teaching found in the *Su-wen?*: 'If you are tranquil and free of troubling thoughts, the primal energy will conform. As long as you preserve that energy within, there is no place for illness to enter.'[41]

"Moreover, the essence of preserving the energy within is to keep it replete and secure throughout the entire body—extending to all the three hundred and sixty joints and each of the eighty-four thousand pores of the skin. You must know that this is the ultimate secret of sustaining life.

"P'eng Tsu said, 'Close yourself up in a room where you won't be disturbed. Prepare a mat with bedding that has been warmed and a pillow about three inches high. Lie face upward with your body completely straight. Close your eyes and confine the heart-energy within your breast. Place a goose feather on your nose. When your breathing does not disturb the feather, count three hundred breaths. Once you have reached a state where your ears do not hear and your eyes do not see, cold and heat will no longer discomfort you; the poisonous stings of bees and scorpions will be unable to harm you. Upon attaining the age of three hundred and sixty, you will be very close to becoming a true person.'[42]

"Su Tung-p'o gave the following advice: 'If you are hungry, eat some food, but stop eating before you are full.[43] Take a long, leisurely stroll, until you feel your appetite return, then enter a quiet room and seat yourself in an upright posture. Begin exhaling and inhaling, counting your breaths—from ten to a hundred, from a hundred to a thousand. By the time you have counted a

The Great
Bodhisattva One
Hand (Tōrei)

thousand breaths, your body should be as firm and steady as a rock, your heart as tranquil and motionless as the empty sky.

"'If you continue to sit like this for a long period, your breath will hang suspended. You will no longer inhale or exhale. Your breath will exude in clouds, rise up like mist, from the eighty-four thousand pores of your skin. You will realize with perfect clarity that all the illnesses you have suffered from, each of the countless disorders you have experienced from the beginningless beginning, have all vanished of themselves. You will be like a blind man suddenly regaining his sight who no longer has need to ask others for guidance on his way.

"'What you must do is to cut back on words and devote yourself solely to sustaining your primal energy. Hence, it is said, "Those who wish to strengthen their sight keep their eyes closed. Those who wish to strengthen their hearing avoid sounds. Those who wish to sustain their heart-energy maintain silence."'"[44]

THE SOFT-BUTTER METHOD

"You mentioned a method in which butter is used," I [Hakuin] said. "May I ask you about that?"[45]

Master Hakuyū replied, "When a student engaged in meditation finds that he is exhausted in body and mind because the four constituent elements of his body are in a state of disharmony, he should gird up his spirit and perform the following visualization:

"Imagine that a lump of soft butter, pure in color and fragrance and the size and shape of a duck egg, is suddenly placed on the top of your head. As it begins to slowly melt, it imparts an exquisite sensation, moistening and saturating your head within and without. It continues to ooze down, moistening your shoulders, elbows, and chest; permeating lungs, diaphragm, liver, stomach, and bowels; moving down the spine through the hips, pelvis, and buttocks.

"At that point, all the congestions that have accumulated within the five organs and six viscera, all the aches and pains in the abdomen and other affected parts, will follow the heart as it sinks downward into the lower body. As it does, you will distinctly hear a sound like that of water trickling from a higher to a lower place. It will move lower down through the lower body, suffusing the legs with beneficial warmth, until it reaches the soles of the feet, where it stops.

"The student should then repeat the contemplation. As his vital energy flows downward, it gradually fills the lower region of the body, suffusing it with penetrating warmth, making him feel as if he were sitting up to his navel in a hot bath filled with a decoction of rare and fragrant medicinal herbs that have been gathered and infused by a skilled physician.

"Inasmuch as all things are created by the mind, when you engage in this contemplation, the nose will actually smell the marvelous scent of pure, soft butter; your body will feel the exquisite sensation of its melting touch. Your body and mind will be in perfect peace and harmony. You will feel better and enjoy greater health than you did as a youth of twenty or thirty. At this time, all the undesirable accumulations in your vital organs and viscera will melt away. Stomach and bowels will function perfectly. Before you know it, your skin will glow with health. If you continue to practice the contemplation with diligence, there is no illness that cannot be cured, no virtue that cannot be acquired, no level of sagehood that cannot be reached, no religious practice that cannot be mastered. Whether such results appear swiftly or slowly depends only upon how scrupulously you apply yourself.

"I was a sickly youth, in much worse shape than you are now. I experienced ten times the suffering you have endured. The doctors finally gave up on me. I explored hundreds of cures on my own, but none of them brought me any relief. I turned to the gods for help. Prayed to the deities of both heaven and earth, begging them for their subtle, imperceptible assistance. I was marvelously blessed. They extended me their support and protection. I came upon this wonderful method of soft-butter contemplation. My joy knew no bounds. I immediately set about practicing it with total and single-minded determination. Before even a month was out, my troubles had almost totally vanished. Since that time, I've never been the least bit bothered by any complaint, physical or mental.

"I became like an ignoramus, mindless and utterly free of care. I was oblivious to the passage of time. I never knew what day or month it was, even whether it was a leap year or not. I gradually lost interest in the things the world holds dear, soon forgot completely about the hopes and desires and customs of ordinary men and women. In my middle years, I was compelled by circumstance to leave Kyoto and take refuge in the mountains of Wakasa Province. I lived there nearly thirty years, unknown to my fellow men. Looking back on that period of my life, it seems as fleeting and unreal as the dream-life that flashed through Lu-sheng's slumbering brain.[46]

"Now I live here in this solitary spot in the hills of Shirakawa, far from all human habitation. I have a layer or two of clothing to wrap around my withered old carcass. But even in midwinter, on nights when the cold bites through the thin cotton, I don't freeze. Even during the months when there are no mountain fruits or nuts for me to gather, and I have no grain to eat, I don't starve. It is all thanks to this contemplation.

"Young man, you have just learned a secret that you could not use up in a whole lifetime. What more could I teach you?"

TAKING LEAVE OF HAKUYŪ

Master Hakuyū sat silently with his eyes closed. I thanked him profusely, my own eyes glistening with tears, and then bade him farewell. The last vestiges of light were lingering in the topmost branches of the trees as I left the cave and made my way slowly down the mountain. Suddenly, I was stopped in my tracks by the *clop clop* of wooden clogs striking the stony ground and echoing up from the sides of the valley. Half in wonder, half in disbelief, I peered apprehensively around to see the figure of Master Hakuyū coming toward me in the distance.

When he was near enough to speak, he said, "No one uses these mountain trails. It's easy to lose your way. You might have trouble getting back, so I'll take you partway down." A skinny wooden staff grasped in his hand, high wooden clogs on his feet, he walked on ahead of me, talking and laughing. He moved nimbly and effortlessly over rugged cliffs and steep mountainside, covering the difficult terrain with the ease of someone strolling through a well-kept garden. After a league or so, we came to the mountain stream. He said if I followed it I would have no trouble finding my way back to the village of Shirakawa. With what seemed a look of sadness, he then turned and began to retrace his steps.

Again, I pressed my palms together and bowed my head low in thanks. I stood there motionless, watching as Master Hakuyū made his way up the mountain trail, marveling at the strength and vigor of his step. He moved with such light, unfettered freedom, as if he were one who had transcended this world, had sprouted wings, and was flying up to join the ranks of immortal sages. Gazing at him, my heart was filled with respect, and with a touch of envy as well. I also felt a pang of regret, knowing that never again in this lifetime would I be able to encounter and learn from a man such as this.

The Benefits of Introspective Meditation

I went directly back to Shōin-ji. There I devoted myself to Introspective Meditation, practicing it over and over on my own. In

less than three years—witho
or moxacautery—the illnesses t.
cleared up of themselves. What is
I experienced the immense joy of gro
boring through and penetrating to the
to-believe, hard-to-penetrate, hard-to-grasp
koans that I had never before been able to ge.
all. I attained countless small satoris as well, which
ing about waving my hands in the air in mindless da
knew for the first time that Zen master Ta-hui had n.
deceiving me when he had written about experiencing eig. ..n
great satoris and countless small ones.

In the past, I used to wear two and even three layers of *tabi*,
but the soles of my feet still always felt as though they were soak-
ing in tubs of ice. Now, even in the third month, the coldest time
of year, I didn't need even a single pair.[47] I no longer required a
brazier to keep myself warm. I am more than eighty years old this
year, but even now I never suffer from the slightest indisposition.
Surely all of this is due to the lingering benefits I enjoy from
having practiced the wonderful secret technique of Introspective
Meditation.

EPILOGUE

Even thinking about it now, the tears trickle down my leathery
old cheeks—I just can't help it.[48] Four or five years ago, I had a
dream. Master Hakuyū had come all the way from the hills of
Shirakawa to visit me here at Shōin-ji. We spent a whole night
laughing and talking together. I felt so happy that the following
morning I told the monks living at the temple all about it. They
bowed and pressed their palms together in attitudes of worship.
"Good! Good!" they said. "Maybe it will come to pass. Perhaps

become reality. If Master Hakuyū did come here,
d be a great honor for the temple.

"You turned eighty this year, master, but your mind and body are both still strong and vigorous. You teach us and extend your help to other students far and wide. Isn't it all thanks to Master Hakuyū? Let one or two of us go to Kyoto and invite him to visit Shōin-ji. He could live here at the temple. We could provide for his needs through our begging."

A feeling of elation passed through the brotherhood. Plans began to be laid. Then a monk stepped forward. "Hold on," he said, laughing. "You're making the mistake of 'marking the side of a moving boat to show where the sword fell in.' I'm sorry to have to be the one to tell you this, but Master Hakuyū, the person you are talking about, is no longer alive. He died this past summer."

The monks clapped their hands in astonishment.

"You shouldn't repeat idle rumors like that!" I said, admonishing the monk. "Hakuyū is no ordinary man. He is one of the immortal sages who just happens to walk the earth. How could such a man die?"

"Unfortunately, that was his undoing. It is because he trod the earth that he met his death. Last summer, it seems he was walking in the mountains and came to the edge of a deep ravine. It was more than a hundred yards to the other side. He tried to leap across, but he didn't make it. He fell to the rocks below. His death was lamented by villagers far and near."

The monk, his story completed, stood there with a forlorn look on his face. I found my own eyes shedding copious tears.

Don't be saying old Hakuin, half dead and gasping out his final breaths, has recklessly scribbled out a long tissue of groundless nonsense hoping to hoodwink superior students. What I've put down here is not intended for those who possess spiritual powers of the first order—the kind of superior seeker who is awakened at a single blow from his master's mallet. But if dull, plodding oafs like me—the kind of people who will suffer from illness as I did—get a look at this book, read and contemplate its meaning, they should surely be able to obtain a little help from it. In fact, after giving the matter more consideration, I think perhaps the benefit will not necessarily be small. In any event, the main thing—what we must all cherish and revere—is the secret method of Introspective Meditation.

In the spring of the seventh year of the Hōreki era [1757], I composed a work in Japanese that I called *Idle Talk on a Night Boat*. In it, I set forth the essential principles of the meditation. Ever since then, people of all kinds—monks, nuns, laymen, laywomen—have told me how, when the odds were stacked ten to one against them, they were saved from the misery of grave and incurable illnesses owing to the wonderful benefits of Introspective Meditation. They have come to me here at Shōin-ji in numbers I cannot even count to thank me in person.

Two or three years ago, a young man—he must have been about twenty-two or twenty-three—showed up at the temple asking to see me. When I stepped out to greet him, I was taken aback by the great bundle of presents—including several gold coins—he had brought for me. He bowed his head to the ground. "I am so-and-so from Matsuzaka in Ise Province," he said. "About six years ago, I came down with a serious ailment, which I found impossible to cure. I tried all the secret remedies I knew, but none of them had any effect whatever. All the physicians I consulted wrote me off as a hopeless case. It seemed then that there was nothing left for me to do except await the end. A wonderful thing then happened. I chanced to read *Idle Talk on a Night Boat*. As best I could with my meager abilities, I began to practice the secret technique of Introspective Meditation on my own. What a blessing it was! Little by little, my energy began to return. Today I am restored to perfect health. I can't tell you how happy and thankful I felt. I was dancing on air! Since it had all come about because I happened upon *Idle Talk on a Night Boat*, there was nowhere I could go—no physician or healer to whom I could express my gratitude. Fortunately, however, as I was mulling what I should do, I heard a vague rumor that you, Master Hakuin, were the author of *Idle Talk on a Night Boat*. Immediately, I wanted to see your revered countenance so I could express my profound gratitude to you in person. On the pretext of transacting some business in Edo, I traveled all the way from Ise Province to see you. This is the happiest moment of my entire life. Nothing could exceed it."

As I listened to him relate the details of his story, can you imagine the happiness this old monk also felt?

I'm only afraid that other people, when they read this work, will clap their hands and break into great peals of laughter. Why is that?

> *A horse calmly chewing its fodder*
> *Disturbs a man at his midday nap.*[49]

Written on the Buddha's birthday, the third year of Meiwa [1766]

112

Preface to Idle Talk on a Night Boat

COMPILED BY HUNGER AND COLD, THE MASTER OF POVERTY HERMITAGE[1]

IN SPRING of the seventh year of the Hōreki era [1757], a Kyoto bookseller by the name of Ogawa dispatched an urgent letter to the Shōin-ji in far-off Suruga Province. It was addressed to the monks who attended master Kokurin [Hakuin]:

> It has come to my attention that there is lying buried among your teacher's unpublished writings a manuscript bearing some such title as *Idle Talk on a Night Boat*. It is said to contain many secret techniques for disciplining the vital *ki*-energy, sustaining the seminal force, filling the defensive energy and nutritive blood to repletion, and in particular for attaining long life—in short, it contains the ultimate essentials of "refining the elixir" that were known to the divine sages.
>
> Superior men of today who have a strong interest in such matters would be as eager to read it as someone in the midst of a parching drought would be seeking signs of rain. Zen monks may occasionally be permitted to make copies of the manuscript for

Monk
on a
Bridge

their own private use, but they keep them hidden away as their most precious possessions, and they never show them to others.

To respond to the yearnings of these superior religious seekers, I would like to have the manuscript printed and ensure that it will be passed on to future generations. I have heard that your teacher, as he grows older, takes a constant pleasure in helping his fellow men. Surely if he believed publishing this work would benefit people, he would not refuse my request.

My fellow attendant and I showed Mr. Ogawa's letter to the master. As he read it, his mouth formed into a faint smile. We took this as a sign of consent. We got out the old box containing the manuscripts, but when we opened it, we found more than half of the pages were already gone, digested inside the bellies of the bookworms. The monks in the master's assembly thereupon brought together the copies they had made. From them, we were able to compile a fair copy of the text. In all, it came to some fifty pages of writing. We wrapped it right up and sent it off to Mr. Ogawa in Kyoto. Being slightly senior to the other monks, I was urged to write something to introduce the work to readers and explain how it came to be written. I accepted the task without hesitation.

The master has resided at Shōin-ji for almost forty years now. Monks intent on plumbing the Zen depths have been coming to him ever since the time he first hung up his travel pack to stay. From the moment they set foot inside the gates, they willingly endured the venomous slobber the master spewed at them. They welcomed the stinging blows from his stick. The thought of leaving never even entered their minds. Some stayed for ten, even twenty years, totally indifferent to the possibility they might have to lay down their lives at Shōin-ji and become dust under the temple pines. They were, to a man, towering giants of the Zen forest, dauntless heroes to all mankind.

They took shelter in old houses and abandoned dwellings, in ancient temple halls and ruined shrines. Their lodgings were spread over an area five or six leagues around Shōin-ji. Hunger awaited them in the morning. Freezing cold lurked for them at night. They sustained themselves on greens and wheat chaff. Their ears were assaulted by the master's deafening shouts and abuse. Their bones were hammered by furious blows from his fists and stick. What they saw furrowed their foreheads in disbelief. What they heard bathed their bodies in cold sweat. There were scenes a demon would have wept to see. Sights that would have moved a devil to press his palms together in pious supplication.

When they first arrived at Shōin-ji, they possessed the beauty of a Sung Yü or Ho Yen, their complexions glowing with radiant health. But before long, they were as thin and haggard as a Tu Fu or Chia Tao, their pallid skin drawn taut over their bony cheeks. You would have thought you were witnessing Ch'ü Yüan at the river's edge, about to leap to his death.[2]

Would a single one of these monks have remained at Shōin-ji even a moment if he had not been totally devoted to his quest, grudging neither his health nor life itself?

In their utter dedication to their training, these monks cast aside all restraint and pushed themselves past the limits of endurance. Some injured their lungs, causing them to be parched of their natural fluid; this led to painful ailments in the abdominal region, which became chronic and serious and difficult to cure.

The master observed their suffering with deep concern and compassion. For days, he went around with a worried look on his face. Unable to suppress his feelings any longer, he finally "descended from the cloudy summit" and began to explain the essential secrets of Introspective Meditation to his students: he was like an elderly mother wringing the last drops of stinking milk from her paps to nourish a beloved son.

He said: "If one of you superior religious seekers who are vigorously engaged in Zen training finds that his heart-fire is mounting upward against the natural flow, draining him physically and mentally and upsetting the proper balance of his five organs, he may attempt to correct his condition by means of acupuncture, moxacautery, or medicines. But even if he could enlist the aid of a physician as illustrious as Hua T'o, he would find it impossible to cure himself.[3]

"Fortunately, I have been entrusted with a secret technique, perfected by the divine sages, for returning the elixir to the sea of vital energy below the navel. I want you to try this technique. If you do, you will see its marvelous efficacy for yourselves: it will appear to you like a bright sun breaking through a veil of cloud and mist.

"If you decide to practice this secret technique you should, for the time being, cease your practice of zazen. Set aside your koan study. First of all, it is important that you get a sound night's sleep. Before you close your eyes, lie on your back, put your legs together, and stretch them out straight, pushing downward as hard as you can with the soles of your feet. Next, draw all your primal energy down into the elixir field, so that it fills the lower body—the space below the navel, down through the lower back and legs, to the soles of the feet. Periodically observe the following thoughts:

1. This elixir field located in the sea of vital energy, the lower back and legs, the soles of the feet—it is all my true and original face. How can that original face have nose holes?
2. This elixir field located in the sea of vital energy, the lower back and legs, the soles of the feet—it is all the home and native place of my original being. What news or tidings could come from that native place?
3. The elixir field located in the sea of vital energy, the lower

back and legs, the soles of the feet—it is all the Pure Land
of my own mind. How could the splendors of that Pure
Land exist apart from my mind?

4. The elixir field located in the sea of vital energy—it is all
the Amida Buddha of my own self. How could Amida
Buddha preach the Dharma apart from that self?

"Turn these contemplations over and over in your mind. As
you do, the cumulative effect of focusing your thoughts on them
will gradually increase. Before you even realize it, all the primal
energy in your body will concentrate in your lower body, filling
the space from the lower back and legs down to the soles of the
feet. The abdomen below the navel will become taut and dis-
tended—as tight and full as a leather kickball that has never been
used.

"Repeat these contemplations over and over. Perform them
assiduously in the same way. In as little as five to seven days, and
in no more than two or three weeks, all the infirmities that have
been afflicting your vital organs and making you physically and
mentally weak will disappear completely. If by then you are not
totally cured, this old neck of mine is yours for the taking."

The master's students bowed deeply to him, their hearts
filled with joy.

They began to practice as he had instructed them to. Each
one of them experienced for himself the marvelous effects of Introspective Meditation. For some, results came quickly; for others, it took somewhat longer. It depended entirely on how
assiduously they practiced the technique. Almost all experienced
complete recoveries. Their praise of the meditation knew no
bounds.

"Once the infirmity in your hearts is cured," said the master,
"you must not rest content with that. The stronger you become,
the harder you must strive in your practice. The deeper you pene-

trate into enlightenment, the more resolutely you must press
forward.

"When I was a young man taking my first steps along the
religious path, I, too, developed a serious illness. Cure seemed
impossible. The misery I suffered then was ten times greater than
anything you have experienced. I was at the end of my tether.
Didn't know what to do, which way to turn. One thing I was sure
of, however. I'd be better off dying and having done with it. Then
at least I'd be free and no longer troubled by this miserable bag
of skin. Anything was better than going on as I was, wallowing
impotently in that black despair. Yet still I suffered. How I suffered! Then I encountered a wise man who taught me the secret
method of Introspective Meditation. Thanks to him, I was able
to cure myself completely, just like you monks.

"According to this man, Introspective Meditation is the secret method the divine sages employed to prolong their lives and
attain immortality. It enabled those of even mediocre and inferior
ability to live for three hundred years. A person of superior capacity might prolong his life almost indefinitely. I could scarcely contain my joy when I heard him say that. I began to practice the
meditation and continued it faithfully for some three years. Gradually, my body and mind returned to perfect health. My vital
spirits revived. I felt myself grow steadily stronger and more con-
fident.

"It became increasingly clear at this point that even if I did
master the method of Introspective Meditation and lived to be
eight hundred years old like P'eng Tsu, I'd still be no better than
one of those disembodied spirits that guard the dead. I'd be like
an old polecat slumbering away in a comfortable old burrow until,
eventually, I passed away. Why do I say this? Well, has anyone
today ever caught sight of Ko Hung? How about T'ieh Kuai or
Chang Hua or Fei Chang? Or any others who are celebrated for
their longevity? In any event, attaining long life in itself cannot

compare with establishing the Four Great Universal Vows in your heart, constantly working to impart the great Dharma to others, and acquiring the dignified ways of Bodhisattvahood. It cannot compare with realizing the true and invincible Dharma body, which, once attained, is never lost, which is as unborn and undying as the great void—with realizing the great, incorruptible, adamantine body of the Buddhas.

"Later, when I acquired two or three students of my own, men of superior ability who were deeply committed to penetrating the secret depths, I had them practice Introspective Meditation along with their Zen training—just like those countrymen who work their fields and serve and fight in the militia as well. Perhaps thirty years have passed since then. My students have increased, one or two each year. Now they number almost two hundred. Over those three decades, I've had monks come from all over the country. Some of the more zealous pushed themselves too hard in their practice and reached a state of extreme physical and mental exhaustion that rendered them feeble and spiritless. Some were pushed to the brink of madness as the heart-fire rushed upward against the natural flow. Because of concern and compassion for them, I took them aside and imparted to them the secret teaching of Introspective Meditation. It returned them to health almost immediately. Now the deeper they advance into enlightenment, the more assiduous their training becomes.

"I'm more than seventy years of age. But even now, I don't have the slightest trace of illness or infirmity. I still have a good set of sound teeth. My hearing grows more acute with each passing year, along with my sight: I often forget to put on my spectacles at all. I give my regular sermons twice each month without fail. I travel extensively to conduct Zen meetings in answer to teaching requests from all over the country. Three hundred and sometimes five hundred people attend these gatherings. They last for fifty, even seventy, days at a stretch. I set forth my arbitrary views on various sutras and Zen texts the monks select for me. Although I must have conducted fifty or sixty of these meetings, never once have I missed a lecture. I feel more fit and vigorous today, both physically and mentally, than I did when I was in my twenties or thirties. And there is not a doubt in my mind that it is all due to the marvelous effects of Introspective Meditation."

The monks now came and bowed before the master, their eyes wet with tears. "Please, Master Hakuin," they said, "we want you to write down the essentials of Introspective Meditation. If you commit them to paper, you will relieve the suffering of future generations of monks like us when they succumb to the extreme exhaustion and dull spiritlessness of meditation sickness."

Nodding his agreement, the master took up his brush then and there and wrote out a draft. What did he set forth in that draft?

"There is nothing better for sustaining life and attaining longevity than disciplining the body. The secret of disciplining the body is to focus the vital energy in the elixir field located in the sea of vital energy. When vital energy focuses in the elixir field, the vital spirit gathers there. When the vital spirit gathers in the elixir field, the true elixir is produced. When the elixir is produced, the physical frame is strong and firm and the spirit is full and replete. When the spirit is full and replete, long life is assured.

"This corresponds to the secret method perfected by the ancient sages for 'refining the elixir nine times over' and 'returning it to the source.'

"You must know that the elixir is not located apart from the self. The most essential thing is to make the vital energy in the heart descend into the lower body so that it fills the elixir field in the sea of energy.

"Monks of Shōin-ji, if you are assiduous in practicing the essential teachings I have given you and are never remiss, not only will it cure you of meditation sickness and relieve you of fatigue and spiritual torpor; it will also enable those burdened with the mass of years of accumulated doubt and struggling to reach the final crowning matter of the Zen school to experience a joy so intense they will find themselves clapping their hands ecstatically and whooping in fits of laughter. Why?

> *"When the moon reaches the summit,*
> *Shadows disappear from the wall."*[4]

Offering incense and bowing my head to the floor, I respectfully composed this preface on the twenty-fifth of the first month, in the seventh year of the Hōreki era [1757].

Hunger and Cold, the Master of Poverty Hermitage

NOTES

Translator's Introduction

1. *Kabe Soshō. Hakuin Shō Zenshū* 6, pp. 155–6.
2. *Hakuin Zenji Shū*, pp. 397–8.
3. Hakuin's accounts in both *Wild Ivy* and *Goose Grass* have him returning to Daishō-ji to nurse Sokudō several years earlier, in 1708, immediately after his departure from Shōju-an. Here I follow the chronology given in the *Biography*, which in this case seems more plausible.
4. *Spearflowers. (Yabukōji). Hakuin Oshō Zenshū* 5, pp. 324–5.

Chapter 1

1. The Four Great Universal Vows taken by all Bodhisattvas (Buddhist practicers) at the start of their training, embodying the Mahayana ideal of working to assist others to enlightenment at the same time one strives to deepen one's own attainment: "Sentient beings are numberless, I vow to save them. The deluding passions are inexhaustible, I vow to extinguish them. The Dharma gates are manifold, I vow to enter them. The Buddha Way is supreme, I vow to enter it."

    "Entry through the Gate of Nonduality" is explained in the *Vimalakirti Sutra* as attainment of the state of absolute nondifferentiation, which transcends all relative differences such as self and other, being and nonbeing. Hakuin equates the Mind of Enlightenment (*Bodhichitta*), the mind that aspires toward enlightenment, with the Bodhisattva's vows, given above. In *Wild Ivy*, and elsewhere in his writings, he explains the Mind of Enlightenment as helping others by giving them the "gift of the Dharma"—that is, teaching them and assisting them to attain enlightenment.

2. Tz'u-ming is a posthumous name of the Chinese priest Shih-shuang Ch'u-yüan (986–1039), who studied under Fen-yang Shan-chao in Fen-yang, modern-day Shansi. "East of the river" refers to the area east of the Yellow River in southwest Shansi. The story of Tz'u-ming's dedication to his pursuit of enlightenment held special significance for Hakuin (see Chapter 1, note 42). In *Goose Grass*, Hakuin describes how he found this passage inscribed in the margin of a printed edition of *Spurring Students through the Zen Barrier* (*Hakuin Zenji Shū*, p. 398).

3. *Kenshō*, "seeing into your (true) nature"—signifying enlightenment, or satori—is sometimes formulated as *kenshō jōbutsu*, "seeing into your nature and attaining Buddhahood," where the two terms are virtually synonymous. The *Hsüeh-mo lun* (*Treatise on the Dharma Pulse*), a work traditionally attributed to the first Zen patriarch, Bodhidharma, contains the words, "If you want to master the path of the Buddha, you must first of all achieve kenshō."

4. Kumasaka Chōhan was a master thief of late Heian Japan who plied his trade as a member of the Buddhist priesthood. He is the subject of the No play *Kumasaka*.

5. "Eight schools" is a general reference signifying all schools of Japanese Buddhism.

6. *Silent illumination* (*mokushō*) is a term usually reserved to characterize the Sōtō tradition, which stresses the practice of zazen alone, without the use of koans. When Hakuin inveighs against "silent illumination" Zen, portraying it as "lifeless sitting," "do-nothing" Zen, and the like, his condemnation can generally be understood to encompass all contemporary teachings, including not only those of the Sōtō school but also the Nembutsu Zen of the Ōbaku tradition, and especially the "Unborn" (*Fushō*) teaching of his own Rinzai lineage, which was enjoying considerable success at the time. In Hakuin's view, all these approaches to practice were culpable for not demanding that the student focus his effort single-mindedly on the active pursuit of the kenshō experience.

7. "Doing nothing is the person of true nobility" (*buji kore kinin*) is a saying from the *Record of Lin-chi*, descriptive of the purposeless activity that characterizes the fully enlightened person. Hakuin uses it pejoratively here to criticize the priests for merely mouthing Lin-chi's words without having attained the truth contained in them.

He uses *doing nothing* (*buji*) and similar terms to disparage those (in particular, followers of Bankei Yōtaku's Unborn teaching) who adopt what he considers a complacent, quietistic approach to practice. Elsewhere in his writings, Hakuin has priests such as those described here telling students that "having no thoughts, having no-mind is in itself the highest level attainable in Zen. The slightest impingement of thought creates karma that will consign you to the three evil paths . . . [so you should] not seek Buddhahood, not preach the Dharma" (*Lingering Light from Precious Mirror*, p. 233). Also, "Whatever you do, you must never seek Buddha or Dharma. Do nothing throughout the twenty-four hours of the day, just remain in a state of no-mind and no-thought. As long as you do that, you are Buddhas, just as you are." *Goose Grass* (*Hakuin Zenji Shū*), p. 362.

8. The wooden fish, or *mokugyō*, is a hollow, round wooden drum beaten while chanting Buddhist texts. *"Namu kara tan nō tora ya ya"* are the opening phrases of the *Dharani of the Great Compassionate One* (*Daihi shu*), a text that was recited daily in most Zen temples. Being primarily phonetic transcriptions from the Sanskrit, *Dharani* are largely unintelligible to the person reciting them. Here Hakuin is apparently assigning equivalents from colloquial Japanese to the syllables of the *Dharani*, so as to make the priest say something like: "I place full trust in [*Namu*] my surplice [*kara*], that's all I need to do [reading *tan nō* as *tarunō*]!" A *kara* or *rakusu*, a biblike piece of cloth worn over the chest, hanging around the neck as a kind of abbreviated surplice or *kasa* (*kasaya*), is a symbol of the priesthood. Hakuin uses the phrase "*Tora* [tiger] *ya ya* [exclamations of terror]" as a reply to the priest, saying, "You'd better watch out. Priests who teach without having experienced kenshō face a future existence more terrifying than a hungry tiger."

Although the following verse is apparently of Chinese origin, its provenance is unknown.

9. In this paragraph and the next, the meaning turns on the Japanese words *shukke* ("house-leaver") and *zaike* ("householder," or layperson). What is important, Hakuin says, is not whether you have been ordained or not but whether you have achieved kenshō (satori).

10. These are five evil acts (parricide, matricide, killing a saint, injuring the body of a Buddha, and causing disunity in the Sangha, or reli-

gious community), commission of which consigns the perpetrator to the worst regions of hell.

11. The *Ten-Phrase Kannon Sutra* (*Jikku Kannon-gyō; Emmei Jikku Kannon-gyō*), consisting of only forty-two Chinese characters in ten phrases, appears in *Records of the Buddhas and Patriarchs* (*Fo-tsu tung-chi*), a Chinese Buddhist work dating from the southern Sung dynasty. It seems to have first come into general use as a short recitation text in Japan during Hakuin's lifetime. According to a story told in Tōrei's *Biography* (1745, Age 60), Hakuin began propagating the sutra at the request of a high-ranking official named Inoue Hyōma. After falling into a swoon, Hyōma had received a direct communication from Yama, the king of hell, informing him that Hakuin was the only person alive capable of popularizing the sutra. A large portion of *Goose Grass* is devoted to stories of people saved from various difficult situations thanks to the miraculous effects caused by constant recitation of the *Ten-Phrase Kannon Sutra*.

 The Hell of Screams is the fourth of the Eight Hot Hells.

12. *Tales of Cause and Effect* (*Inga Monogatari*), by Suzuki Shōsan (1579–1655), is a collection of stories, similar to the one given here, compiled and published in 1654 by Shōsan's disciples. The story told here is not found in the collection.

13. It should be pointed out that, at this date, when Hakuin would have been in his early thirties, it is unlikely he would have been invited to a temple to teach.

14. People believed to be bewitched or possessed by the spirit of the wild fox commonly exhibit wildly irrational and often violent behavior.

15. A *shippei* is a lacquered bamboo stick two or more feet long wrapped around the head with wisteria vine. It is carried or kept at hand by a Zen master as a symbol of office and, when necessary, for use on students.

16. Another reference to the "Unborn" (*Fushō*) Zen teaching of the Rinzai priest Bankei Yōtaku (1622–1693), one common formulation of which was: "All things are perfectly taken care of if you just remain in the Unborn Buddha-mind you received at birth from your parents. Do not transform your Buddha-mind into illusory thoughts" (see Waddell, *Unborn: The Life and Teachings of Zen Master Bankei*). Bankei's teaching gained a wide following through-

out the country in the latter part of the seventeenth century and was especially dominant in the areas of central Japan where Hakuin was traveling. Although Hakuin never mentions Bankei by name in his attacks on Unborn Zen, there seems little doubt that—in some instances, at least—he is referring not to followers of Bankei's teachings but to Bankei himself.

17. Hakuin is alluding to the story of Po-chang's fox, the second koan in the *Gateless Barrier* collection. Po-chang was approached by an old man who told him that when he himself had been a Buddhist abbot many lives in the past and someone had asked him whether or not an enlightened person could fall under the sway of cause and effect, his reply, that such a person "did not fall," had doomed him to rebirth for five hundred fox lives.

18. Inari Myōjin, the deity of grains, is represented in the popular mind by its messenger, the white fox.

19. Dogs are supposed to be able to sense the fox spirit, even when it has assumed human form.

20. "With each new life, one forgets the events of one's previous existence" (*kyakushō sokumo*). This phrase, originally from the *Fa-hua ching hsüan-i, chüan* 6, appears in such secular works as the fourteenth-century war chronicle *Taiheiki* (vol. 11): "Though it is said that the things of life are forgotten after death, yet does the karma of a fleeting thought endure for five hundred lives." *The Taiheiki*, translated by Helen McCullough (New York: Columbia University Press, 1959), p. 330. Here the phrase seems to carry a similar nuance and stresses the importance of taking advantage of the rare opportunity of human birth to grasp the principle of karmic cause and effect through kenshō, or satori. Cf. *Goose Grass, Hakuin Zenji Shū*, p. 417.

21. Hakuin insinuates that the priests were uneasy because they themselves were followers of the fallen priest's teaching of Unborn Zen.

22. These lines appear in a verse Hakuin had composed some years earlier for a ceremony commemorating the death anniversary of Bodhidharma (Takeuchi, *Hakuin, zuhan kaisetsu*, plate no. 311). They also appear as a "capping phrase" (*jakugo*) in his commentaries on Zen texts (for example, *Dokugo shingyō*). Presumably, they represent his appraisal of the preceding story and contain a criticism of the half-baked priests described in the previous paragraph. The autumn melancholy depicted in the first line evokes the feeling of

worldly impermanence; the second line, the joy and affirmation experienced upon passing through the perception of impermanence
and death and emerging into the enlightened realm of ultimate
wisdom.

23. The statesman and scholar Sugawara Michizane was enshrined at
the Kitano Shrine in Kyoto in 987. He later came to be worshiped
as Kitano Tenjin, patron deity of calligraphy, letters, and culture in
general. Michizane, who died on the twenty-fifth day of the sixth
month, is said to have been born on the twenty-fifth of the second
month. His anniversary is observed on the twenty-fifth of each
month at the main Kitano Tenjin Shrine in Kyoto and at the countless smaller Tenjin shrines throughout Japan. A Tenjin shrine and
sacred grove were located at the Sainen-ji, a Ji sect temple just behind Hakuin's family home in Hara. Since the ox is the messenger
of Tenjin, Tenjin became known, especially in eastern Japan, as
"Ushi Tenjin," the Ox deity.

24. Nichigon Shōnin (n.d.). According to a note in Tōrei's draft *Biography*, Nichigon was a preacher of great power who made the rounds
of Nichiren temples in eastern Japan delivering sermons to the
faithful.

25. Nichiren Shōnin (1222–1282), founder of the Nichiren sect. The letters of instruction Nichiren wrote to his followers are translated in
Letters of Nichiren, translated by Burton Watson and Philip Yampolsky (New York: Columbia University Press, 1996). The *Biography* has Nichigon lecturing on Chih-i's *Great Concentration and
Insight* (*Mo-ho chih-kuan*).

26. The *Tenjin Sutra*, consisting of roughly a hundred Chinese characters, was probably composed around the beginning of the Edo period. It was printed at the end of textbooks used in *terakoya* schools
during the Edo period to inculcate students with a reverence for
Tenjin. Buddhist in vocabulary but with a verbal meaning that is at
times unclear, it closes with an invocation to Tenjin: "*Namu Ten-
man Daijizai Tenjin*" ("Homage to Tenjin, deity of great freedom,
deity of the Tenmangu Shrine").

27. There seems to be no record of an artist by this name. The archery
game (*hamaya*), a New Year's pastime, involved shooting at small,
round targets that were tossed into the air.

28. Hakuin refers to the *Kannon Sutra* as the *Fumon-bon* (*Chapter of

the Universal Gate), the title it bears in its original setting as part of the *Lotus Sutra*.

29. Suwa was a village not far from Hara. The play in question, about the evangelist Nichiren priest Nisshin Shōnin (1407–1488), known as "Pot-Wearer [*nabe-kaburi*] Nisshin," is probably *Nisshin Shōnin Tokkō Ki* (*The Virtuous Conduct of Nisshin Shōnin*), a work by Chikamatsu Monzaemon that was first performed at the beginning of the Genroku era (1688–1704). The shogun in question was actually not Tokimune but Ashikaga Yoshinori. The formula "*Namu-myōhō-renge-kyō*," "I take refuge in *Myōhō-renge-kyō*" (the full Japanese title of the *Lotus Sutra*), is recited by Nichiren Buddhists in much the same way Pure Land devotees recite the name of Amida Buddha. In the *Lotus Sutra* (*Fumon-bon/Kannon Sutra*), the protection extended by Kannon Bodhisattva to true practicers of the *Lotus* is said to allow them to enter fire without being burned or be washed away in a flood without being drowned.

30. A large number of such anthologies, known as *Kuzō-shi*, appeared during the Edo period. They consist of short poetical quotations from Zen texts and Chinese literature, used by Zen students as source books for *jakugo* or "capping phrases" for koans. It was said to take young monks three years of hard study to master all the phrases. *Goose Grass, Hakuin Zenji Shū*, p. 395.

31. Nyoka, or Nyoka Rōshi, who appears several times in *Wild Ivy*, is generally assumed to be Sokudō Fueki, the priest of the Daishō-ji in Numazu under whom Hakuin studied during his first four years as a monk. Abe Hōshun, however, identifies him as Tōrin Soshō, an elder brother in the Dharma of Hakuin who succeeded Tanrei Soden as priest at Shōin-ji (*Shōju Rōjin Shū*, p. 159). See Chapter 3, note 33.

32. The Five Canonical Books of Confucianism: *Book of Changes, Book of Odes, Book of History, Book of Rites, Spring and Autumn Annals. Wen-hsüan* is a classified compendium of various types of Chinese literature compiled in the sixth century that was widely read and studied in Japan.

33. Kin Shuso (Tōhō Sokin, d. 1729) was a monk of the Tokugen-ji, a small Rinzai temple located next to the Shōin-ji. Zensō-ji is a Rinzai temple in the city of Shimizu, Suruga Province, in the present-day Shizuoka Prefecture. According to Tōrei's *Biography*, Hakuin

was disappointed on arriving at the Zensō-ji to find the monks studying texts instead of practicing zazen. It was the first of many encounters he would have with the "do-nothing" Zen he would later attack for undermining the traditions of koan Zen.

34. The head priest at Zensō-ji, Sen'ei Soen (1659–1726), was lecturing on *The Wind and Moon Collection of Zen Poetry* (*Chiang-hu feng-yüeh chi*), a fourteenth-century collection of verse by priests of the southern Sung and Yuan dynasties. During a suppression of Buddhism in the mid-ninth century, when hundreds of thousands of monks and nuns were returned to lay status, Yen-t'ou Ch'üan-huo (828–887) continued to teach while living as a ferryman at Lake Tung-ting in Hunan. Hakuin discovered the facts surrounding Yen-t'ou's death in a headnote to the text of *Praise of the True School* (*Wu-chia cheng-tsung tsan*), a work containing brief biographies of important priests of the five main schools of Chinese Zen that he found in the temple library. Hakuin's doubts about Yen-t'ou's death cry were finally resolved at the time of his initial satori experience four years later. Although Hakuin was probably not aware of it at the time, some accounts of Yen-t'ou's life explain the death cry as the fulfillment of a promise he had made to his students that he would emit a great Zen shout when he died. In his colophon to the *Biography*, Tōrei praised the loud groan Hakuin uttered when he died as "a final Zen utterance worthy of Yen-t'ou."

35. This is a reference to transmigratory rebirth as a hungry ghost, a fighting demon, or an animal.

36. Sōnen (1298–1356), a son of the Emperor Fushimi, was the abbot of the Seiren-in temple of Kyoto and founder of a school of calligraphy whose style was made standard for official documents during the Edo period. Terai Yōsetsu was a noted contemporary Kyoto calligrapher.

37. Baō Rōjin: Baō Sōchiku (1629–1711). Almost all that is known about Baō comes from Hakuin's writings. Although Baō was a priest and an heir of the Rinzai master Rizan Sōdon, Hakuin praises him for his scholarship and makes no direct mention of his qualities as a religious teacher.

38. *Ekaku,* the name Hakuin received at his ordination, means "Wise Crane." He adopted the name *Hakuin* at the time he assumed the abbotship of Shōin-ji. Baō's words are an ironic comment on Ha-

kuin's traveling companions, who were busy readying themselves to leave (flee) the temple.

39. A note to Tōrei's draft *Biography*, expurgated from the final printed text, explains the reason for Baō's frequent outings "to enjoy himself" in the city of Ōgaki: he was infatuated with a nun named Jukei who lived in the city. A few years after his initial stay at Zuiun-ji, Hakuin returned to nurse Baō during an illness. When Baō had recovered and Hakuin was about to leave, Jukei begged him to stay on. Hakuin agreed, but only on condition that Baō remain confined to his sickbed. Whenever he was well enough to leave it, he was well enough to care for himself. Several days later, Baō and Hakuin appeared at Jukei's door. She scolded Baō, saying, "Now brother Ekaku will leave you." Baō, not comprehending her meaning, just stood smiling at her. Hakuin left the next day. Rikugawa Taiun, *Hakuin Oshō Shōden*, pp. 460–61.

40. Tōrei's *Biography* identifies Onbazan (n.d.) as a son of the Neo-Confucian teacher Kumazawa Banzan (1619–1691), who served as chief minister of the Ikeda daimyo of Okayama.

41. It is not known how long a stick of incense took to burn down in Hakuin's day; those used today take roughly thirty minutes.

42. *Spurring Students through the Zen Barrier* (*Ch'an-kuan ts'e-chin*) is a compilation, with comments, of 110 passages from Zen and other Buddhist texts relating to Zen practice by the noted Ming priest Yün-ch'i Chu-hung, whose advocacy of "Nembutsu Zen" is the subject of severe criticism in Hakuin's writings (for example, "Talks Introductory to Lectures on the Record of Hsi-keng," in Waddell, *Essential Teachings of Zen Master Hakuin*, pp. 47–56). Hakuin had opened the book to a passage titled "Jabbing a Gimlet into His Own Thigh," which described the practice of the Chinese master Tz'u-ming (the same priest Hakuin sets forward at the beginning of *Wild Ivy* as a model for Zen practicers): "When Tz'u-ming, Ta-yu, and Lang-yeh were practicing together under Master Fen-yang, the cold east of the river was so bitter that it kept other students away. Tz'u-ming's dedication to the Way never wavered through the days and nights. To keep himself from falling asleep during the long, icy nights, he jabbed a gimlet in his thigh. Later succeeding Master Fen-yang, he greatly whipped up the winds of the school's true traditions, calling himself the 'Lion west of the river.' "

Spurring Students through the Zen Barrier was first published in Japan in 1656; a reprinting with a preface by Tōrei was made in 1762 by some of Hakuin's students. Hakuin, who first learned of the project when he was handed a newly printed copy of the book, described his feelings in a letter he wrote at the time: "I raised the book up in reverence two or three times, unable to stop the tears flowing down my cheeks. My joy was boundless—I felt like jumping up and dancing around the room. . . . I could have received no greater expression of Dharma gratitude. This book has meant more to me than anything else—even my teachers or my own parents. . . . During my pilgrimage, it was always with me; it never left my side" (quoted in Akiyama Kanji, *Shamon Hakuin,* p. 70).

43. The village of Horado, Mino Province, is in present-day Gifu Prefecture near the city of Mino. Nothing much is known of Nanzen Oshō (Nanzen Keryū), aside from his dates, 1662–1710. The Hofuku-ji was a Rinzai temple.

44. The Taia Sword is a metaphor for *prajna* wisdom: destroying all illusions, it brings the total negation (winter) necessary for absolute affirmation (spring) to emerge. Old Mr. South (Nangyoku Rōjin) is an incarnation of the southern summit star Canopus, which was thought to influence peace, prosperity, and human longevity. The verse contains an allusion from the *Huai-nantzu*: Duke Yang of Lu, engaged in a fierce battle and fearing that night would come before his victory was achieved, raised his spear and shook it at the declining sun, which immediately went backward in the sky. Herbert Giles, *Chinese Biographical Dictionary,* no. 2397.

45. The summer retreat (*ge-ango*) lasts for ninety days.

46. Eshō (also Ishō) Kairyō (Kairyū) (d. 1748). Like Hakuin, Kairyō began religious life as a disciple of Sokudō Fueki at the Daishō-ji in Numazu. He later accompanied Hakuin on many of his travels. Although older than Hakuin, Kairyō came to recognize Hakuin's superior ability, became his student, and eventually received sanction as his heir. He later served as head of the Genryū-ji and Muryō-ji, both located in the vicinity of Hara. Unlike Hakuin, who had been furnished with traveling money by his mother and could help contribute to his upkeep, the penniless Kairyō would be a burden on the temple. Hakuin refers to the older monk as his "younger brother" because he was monastically senior to Kairyō.

47. Banri Shutetsu (1650–1713), abbot of the Jōkō-ji in Obama, served a term as head abbot at the Myōshin-ji, so he was a well-regarded priest of the time. He was fifty-seven when Hakuin visited him. The *Record of Hsi-keng* contains the Zen records of the Chinese master Hsü-t'ang Chih-yü; as the teacher of Daiō Kokushi, founder of the most important line of Rinzai Zen, Hsü-t'ang was deeply venerated in Japanese Zen circles.

48. To reach the city of Matsuyama in the province of Iyō, in the present-day Ehime Prefecture, Hakuin had to cross the Inland Sea to the island of Shikoku. The Shōjū-ji (also read Shōshū-ji) was located near Matsuyama Castle. According to *Goose Grass,* the high-ranking military retainer who invited Hakuin to his residence was a chief minister of the lord of Matsuyama Castle.

49. The monks ask Hakuin to leave the realm of the absolute, where verbal explanation is impossible, and descend to the relative plane so he can explain the two Chinese characters—"old mother-in-law"—he wrote on the back of the scroll. In letting them in on his joke, Hakuin tells them the characters for "old mother-in-law" mean *yome nikui,* or "the daughter-in-law [*yome*] is hateful [*nikui*]"—a foregone conclusion where an "old mother-in-law" is concerned—which also contains the pun "difficult to read" (*yome-nikui*). "Descending below the clouds," a phrase Hakuin was fond of using, indicates a Zen master's leaving the realm of the absolute, where verbal explanations are impossible, and descending into the relative plane and employing expedient means to make it accessible to students. The phrase is originally said to refer to the Taoist immortals who fly through the heavens riding upon clouds; when they desire to walk upon the earth, they cause the clouds to descend.

50. Daigu Sōchiku (1584–1669), a highly respected Myōshin-ji teacher active during the seventeenth century, is most closely associated with the Daian-ji, which he founded in the province of Echizen, in present-day Fukui Prefecture. Given the enormous amount of calligraphy and painting Hakuin produced later on, his realization that the true worth of Daigu's calligraphy lay in its religious qualities rather than in the skillfulness of its brushwork is significant and may have suggested to him how his own artistic talent could serve a religious end. In his account of this episode in *Goose Grass,* Hak-

133

uin says the calligraphy was by Ungo Kiyō (1582–1659), another Myōshin-ji priest and contemporary of Daigu.

51. The *Three Teachings of the Buddha Patriarchs* (*Fo-tsu san-ching*), a
Ming collection of three independent works—the *Sutra of Forty-
two Sections,* the *Sutra of the Buddha's Final Instruction,* and *Kuei-
shan's Stick of Encouragement*—contains basic teachings for the use
of students engaged in meditation practice. The quotation in question occurs in section 26 of the *Sutra of Forty-two Sections:* "A person following the Way is like a log in a river, floating along in the
current. If it touches neither bank, is not taken up by men, is not
obstructed by gods or demons, is not held back in the swirls and
eddies, and is not corrupted by rot and decay, it will surely find its
way into the great sea."

   In Tōrei's *Biography* (1706, Age 21), Hakuin gives as his reason
for visiting Shōjū-ji some Zen lectures being given there by the
priest Itsuzen Gijin on *The Three Teachings of the Buddha Patriarchs.*

52. According to Tōrei's *Biography* (1707, Age 22), Hakuin was working
on the Mu koan at this time.

53. These are sites along the Inland Sea in the vicinity of the modern
city of Kobe celebrated for their historical associations and scenic
beauty.

54. Kanzan Egen (1277–1360), founder of the Myōshin-ji in Kyoto.
Hakuin greatly respected and revered Kanzan for the extreme aus-
terity of his life and the uncompromising severity of his teaching
style. Hakuin refers to him by one of his posthumous Kokushi, or
"National Master," titles: Daijō Shōō. The story does not seem to
have a written source.

55. Hakuin probably discovered this passage from the *Larger Prajna-
paramita Sutra* among the sutra texts in *Spurring Students through
the Zen Barrier:* "A voice arose in midair declaring to the Bodhisattva Sadapralapa or Ever-Weeping, 'As you travel eastward from
here in your search for wisdom, your mind should harbor no aver-
sion to fatigue. Do not think of sleep or food or drink. Be oblivious
of day and night. Have no fear of heat or cold. Do not allow your
thoughts to scatter aimlessly within or without in search of things.
When you walk, do not look to the left or right, do not look forward
or backward, up or down, or in any other direction."

56. This monk is identified a few paragraphs later as Chō Jōza, who

may be the same person as Shuchō Jōza, a senior priest at Eigan-ji mentioned in *Goose Grass*. In the *Biography* (1707, Age 22), Tōrei has Hakuin visiting Chō Shuso, a student of the Ōbaku master Egoku Dōmyō, at the Tokugen-ji in Hara the year before the Eigan-ji meeting and says he accompanied Chō the following spring to the Eigan-ji lecture-meeting.

The Eigan-ji in Takada, Echigo Province (present-day Niigata Prefecture), was the family temple of the Toda clan, the hereditary daimyos of Echigo and lords of Takada Castle. Egoku Dōmyō (1632–1721), whom Hakuin himself would visit a few years later, was an heir of the Chinese Ōbaku master Mu-an Hsing-t'ao and one of the most prominent of the Japanese priests who joined the Ōbaku school soon after it was introduced from Ming China during the second half of the seventeenth century. *The Eye of Men and Gods* (*Jen-t'ien yen-mu*), a Sung work, sets forth the basic teaching styles of the five schools of Chinese Zen in passages selected from the sayings and verses of their principal figures.

57. Yen-t'ou's death cry had caused Hakuin to doubt the efficacy of Zen training several years before. Hakuin describes this enlightenment experience in somewhat greater detail in *Orategama* (*Zen Master Hakuin: Selected Writings*, pp. 117–18). The words "mind and body dropped completely away" (*shinjin datsuraku*) that appear here and elsewhere in *Wild Ivy* are closely associated with Sōtō school founder Dōgen Kigen, who used them to express his own enlightenment experience. In the *Goose Grass* account of the enlightenment at Eigan-ji, the full utterance Dōgen is said to have made—"*shinjin datsuraku, datsuraku shinjin*": "mind and body dropped away, dropped away mind and body"—is used. *Hakuin Zenji Shū*, p. 402.

58. Kyōsui Edan (d. 1743). Hakuin refers to him as "One of my monks, Zen man Dan" (*shinanko Dan Zennin*). The unusual term *shinanko* is clarified in the account Hakuin gives of this exchange in *Goose Grass* (*Hakuin Zenji Shū*, pp. 402–3), where he refers to Dan as an assistant serving under his direction in the residence hall. Kyōsui began his study with Kogetsu Zenzai in Kyushu; he later received Dharma sanction from Shōju Rōjin (*Hakuin Oshō Shōden*, pp. 70–74). It is worth noting that he is serving as Hakuin's assistant even though he was probably quite a bit older. The Rinzai-ji was located in Sumpu, the modern city of Shizuoka.

59. Bandō refers to the region of east central Honshu surrounding the city of Edo—more or less equivalent to the Kantō district—regarded by the people of the Kyoto-Osaka area as culturally backward and its inhabitants rough and ill-mannered. A Bandō accent would have a loud, vehement quality and a harsh, gruff provincial ring.

60. Here Dan uses the word *umasuteba* (a place, usually located on the outskirts of a town or village, where the carcasses of workhorses and oxen were buried): "They seem to think this is an *umasuteba*."

61. Dōju Sōkaku (1679–1730). Sōkaku (also referred to as Kaku) served as a tea attendant at Iiyama Castle as a young boy. He is said to have entered religious life and become a student of Shōju Rōjin at the instigation of Fuhaku Koji (Layman Fuhaku: Nakano Shichizaemon), a wealthy sake brewer of Iiyama and a longtime disciple of Shōju who later formed a close friendship with Hakuin. A fuller description of Sōkaku that appears in *Goose Grass* (*Hakuin Zenji Shū*, p. 402) helps explains why the temple priests were so anxious to send him somewhere else: "He looked to be thirty or forty years of age, a veteran monk wearing a tattered robe and with a generally ragged look about him. . . . He didn't even know the proper etiquette for making his request but just boomed out in a loud voice that he wanted to stay at the temple."

62. Etan Zōsu: Dōkyō Etan (1642–1721), better known as Shōju Etan or Shōju Rōjin, "The Old Man of Shōju-an Hermitage." Born the natural son of Sanada Nobuyuki, the lord of Matsushiro in Shinano Province, Shōju was adopted and raised by Matsudaira Tadatomo inside Iiyama Castle. He is said to have displayed an early aptitude for religion and to have experienced a great enlightenment in his fifteenth year, occasioned by a sudden tumble down a flight of stairs. At eighteen, he accompanied his stepfather to Edo, where he was ordained by Shidō Munan at the Tōhoku-an hermitage; a year later, he received Munan's certification of enlightenment. After a six-year pilgrimage, during which he studied with teachers in northeastern Japan, he returned to Munan. He was offered, but refused, the abbotship of a large new temple and remained with Munan at Tōhoku-an until the latter's death in 1676. He then returned to Iiyama, spending the rest of his life living and teaching at the Shōju-an hermitage. An unpublished religious biography of

Shōju compiled by Tōrei was later used by the Meiji master Imagita Kōsen in writing a biography titled *Shōju Rōjin Sūanroku,* published in 1877. Dōkyō Etan Zenji, Shōju's Zen master title, was a title of respect used by his Dharma heirs and was not formally awarded to him. The rank of Daiichiza, or First Monk, was given posthumously by the Myōshin-ji in 1819, honoring the one-hundredth anniversary of his death.

63. Chao-chou's Mu, case 1 of *The Gateless Barrier;* often the first koan given to beginning Zen students.

64. These are the names of "difficult-to-pass" (*nantō*) koans, difficult, complicated koans that Hakuin says should be assigned during post-satori practice.

65. Hakuin's fullest mention of "closed-barrier" (*kansa*) Zen, which he championed as the authentic tradition of the Zen school, is found in *Goose Grass,* where it is described as centered in the study of what he calls "difficult to pass" (*nantō;* the preceding note) koans under a qualified master: "Closed-barrier Zen is the only true Zen. Without closed barriers, teachers will be unable to produce genuine students. Without genuine students, there is no way to transmit the true Dharma to future generations, and the authentic traditions will fall to earth" (*Hakuin Zenji Shū,* p. 390).

66. In Hakuin's account of this incident in *Goose Grass,* he says that a "madwoman" (*kyōjin*) suddenly rushed up to him and began beating him savagely about the head with a broom. He "fell to the ground and remained there unconscious for more than an hour." *Hakuin Zenji Shū,* p. 407.

67. Narasawa, one of five hamlets that make up the village of Iiyama, is described as being "a hedgerow away from the Shōju-an hermitage," which was located in the hamlet of Kamikura (*Shōju Rōjin Shū,* p. 362).

68. The religious standpoint of Hinayana, or Lesser Vehicle, Buddhism, represented by the figures of the Shravaka, or Voice-Hearer, who aspires to the stage of Arhat, or Sage, and the Pratyeka, or Private, Buddha, who gains enlightenment through his own efforts and for himself alone, are unacceptable to Hakuin because they do not, like the Bodhisattva, their counterpart in the Mahayana tradition, devote themselves to assisting others to enlightenment. The admonishment in the final sentence of the paragraph, which Hak-

uin says the Buddha delivered to his disciples, appears throughout Hakuin's writings. Its source has not been traced.

As Hakuin quotes from Shōju throughout the rest of this section, he is obviously mixing in elements of his own (for example, The Sound of One Hand), making it sometimes impossible to distinguish between his words and Shōjus̀. For the sake of clarity, I have made Hakuin the speaker.

69. Here "final difficult barriers" (saigo nojūkan) are apparently koans Hakuin refers to as difficult-to-pass (see p. 74, below; also Goose Grass (Hakuin Zenji Shū, p. 426). However on p. 38, the context clearly suggests a barrier (barriers) after the nantō-koans.

70. These lines appear at the end of The Precious Mirror Samadhi (Pao-tsung san-mei), a Buddhist poem attributed to the Sōtō teacher Tung-shan Liang-chieh: "Hidden practice, scrupulous application, continued uninterrupted like a fool, like a dunce—that is the essence within the essence."

71. This expression, which may be said to characterize Hakuin's basic approach to Zen study, was one of his favorites and appears in many of his calligraphy inscriptions.

72. The expressions "poison fangs and talons of the Dharma cave" (hok-kutsu no doku sōge) and "vicious, life-robbing talismans" (datsumei no aku shimpu) apparently are unique to Hakuin. They appear throughout his writings, referring to the koans the student must struggle with, and "lose his life to," as he advances toward his goal; usually (but not always; cf. Goose Grass, Hakuin Zenji Shū, pp. 418–19) they refer to the difficult nantō koans encountered during post-satori practice. "Losing his life to them and dying into the Great Death from which the Great Life emerges," the student makes their spiritual powers his own. Hakuin may have taken the expression from a Sung work, Lin-kuan lu, chüan 1, where words that possess an especially vital Zen meaning are described as "talons and fangs of the Dharma cave."

73. Hakuin's remarks in the follow paragraphs roughly parallel a teaching found in the Ta-hui shu, the letters of the Sung priest Ta-hui Tsung-kao. Ta-hui explains to a lay student who is a minister of state how the worldly fortune most people seek easily becomes a curse that can extend over three lifetimes: Worldly success in your present life easily makes you overlook your main, spiritual concern

(i.e., seeing into your true nature), although it may allow you to create sufficient good karma so that you will be reborn into a position of wealth and power in your next life. In that next rebirth, you will have the means to enjoy life and do as you wish, but will accumulate unfavorable karma because you do not perform meritorious acts and deeply reflect on the course of your life. By your next rebirth, all the good karma you had accumulated is now used up, so when you die this time, you fall straightaway into hell. The lesson to be drawn, says Ta-hui, is that you should do everything in your power to take advantage of the rare opportunity of human birth and strive to attain salvation by seeing into your true nature.

74. The Sound of One Hand (*Sekishu no onjō*) is the famous koan Hakuin began using from his sixties on, assigning it to students at the start of their koan study in place of the Mu koan. He is thought to have adapted it from a comment by Hsüeh-tou that is found in Case 18 of the *Blue Cliff Record*: "A single hand does not clap in vain." Hakuin's fullest account of this koan, his reasons for adopting it, and an explanation of its meaning are found in *Spearflowers* (*Yabukōji*). See *Zen Master Hakuin: Selected Writings*, pp. 163–79.

75. The "three evil paths" refers to the three lowest states of existence—those of hell, animals, and hungry spirits. The "eight difficult realms" refers to eight situations of transmigratory rebirth that make it difficult to encounter a Buddha or his teaching and thus break free from samsaric suffering: in the regions of hell, hungry ghosts, and animals; in the northern continent Uttarakuru, where life is pleasant but no Buddha appears; in the heavens, where life is long and easy; as a triple invalid (deaf, dumb, and blind); as a worldly philosopher; or in a period when there is no Buddha in the world.

76. "Put a Stop to All Sounds" (*Issai onjō o tomeyō*) is a koan Hakuin gave students after they passed The Sound of One Hand. Inscriptions he wrote to verify his students' satoris commonly contain the words: "He [or "She"] has broken through my Double Barrier: The Sound of One Hand and Stopping All Sounds." In *Goose Grass* (*Hakuin Zenji Shū*, p. 426), he stresses that the student must not stop after hearing the sound of one hand but must continue on and put a stop to all sounds.

77. A statement on the three kinds of succession (*sanshi no wake*) is

found among the records of the Yuan master Yün-wai Yün-hsiu (*Tsung-men shih-fa lun*, Zokuzō-kyō [Zenshūbu] 21, 1021).

78. Sōkaku actually went on to succeed Shōju as head priest at Shōju-an and lived another twenty-five years.

79. The Kasaga Shrine in the city of Nara is one of the most important in Japan. Gedatsu Shōnin (the posthumous title of the Hossō scholar-priest Jōkei, 1132–1186) lived at a temple on Mount Kasagi, northeast of Nara. The Buddha Kuruson (Sanskrit, *Krakucchandha*) is said to have been the first of the thousand Buddhas to appear in the course of the present age. Hakuin frequently quotes this story to stress the primary importance for a priest to possess the "Mind of Enlightenment" (*Bodhichitta*). He describes the terror he felt when he first read this story in *A Gathering of Sand and Pebbles* (*Shaseki-shū*), a collection of Buddhist stories compiled by Mujū Ichien in 1279. Although several passages in *A Gathering of Sand and Pebbles* stress the importance of the Mind of Enlightenment (for example, *kan* 9: "No matter how much a person may study and practice, if any attachment to fame or profit remains in his mind, he will enter the paths of evil"), the version Hakuin gives here does not appear.

80. Myōe Shōnin (1173–1232) is a famous scholar-priest of the Kegon school. His temple, Kōzan-ji, is located at Toganoo, west of Kyoto. For Hakuin, Myōe would represent the Mahayana position, as against Gedatsu Shōnin's Hinayana, or Two Vehicle, standpoint.

81. It appears that Hakuin wrote the initial part of this epilogue when he completed the first chapter of *Wild Ivy* and the rest of it later after finishing the remaining chapters.

82. A well-known saying found in a Yuan work, the *Lu ts'ai-lang*, by Kuan Han-ch'ing, probably derived from a similar statement in the *Book of Rites*.

Chapter 2

1. These are the first two lines of a four-line verse Hakuin composed for a ceremony commemorating the death anniversary of Bodhidharma: "Plenty of greens in my kitchen, but the chopping blade won't cut; / Stoking the temple stove with autumn leaves, the fire

tongs are busy; / A meager offering, true and authentic, I'm unable to present. / The blue-eyed monk from India [Bodhidharma] is secretly heartbroken" (*Poison Stamens in a Thicket of Thorns, Hakuin Oshō Zenshū*, 2, p. 33). The verse, which describes preparations in the temple kitchen for the maigre feast held in observance of the sect founder's death anniversary, probably is an expression of Hakuin's state of mind at this point in his training, when, having just left Shōju, he is about to proceed with post-satori training. Perhaps the lines indicate Hakuin's sense of his unworthiness: although he knows that he possesses a full store of attainment, he finds himself still unable to express it freely. And until he attains this freedom in full awakening, he will be unable to truly requite the immense debt of gratitude he owes the founder of the Zen tradition.

2. It is not known how long a stick of incense took to burn down in Hakuin's day. Those used today burn for roughly thirty minutes.

3. The story of Hakuin's struggle against this ailment is the subject of Chapter 4.

4. Hatsu: Ehatsu Setten (n.d.). The Ryōun-ji was located in Numazu. According to Tōrei's *Biography*, Hakuin went to nurse Nyoka Rōshi toward the end of 1711 and stayed with him until summer of the following year. Nyoka died in the seventh month of 1712. In *Goose Grass*, Hakuin states that he left Shōju because he heard Nyoka was seriously ill and had no one to care for him (*Hakuin Zenji Shū*, p. 411).

5. Jōsan Jakuji (1676–1736), head priest of the Kenkoku-ji, was a Dharma heir of the noted Rinzai master Kengan Zen'etsu. Kengan was the master of Kogetsu Zenzai, whom Hakuin was planning to visit at about this time.

6. Hakuin visited Egoku at the Hōun-ji in Kawachi Province, present-day Osaka Prefecture (see Chapter 1, note 56). According to Tōrei's *Biography* (1713, Age 28), Hakuin sought Egoku's advice on how to integrate the active side of his practice with the meditative side.

7. Hakuin said he visited the Inryō-ji, located in Izumi Province (present-day Osaka Prefecture; about twenty kilometers from Hōun-ji), in 1713 in order to learn about the teaching style of its former abbot and founder, the Sōtō priest Tesshin Dōin (1593–1680). Tesshin studied with the Chinese master Tao-che Ch'ao-yüan (1600–1662?)

in Nagasaki (his fellow students included Egoku Dōmyō and Bankei Yōtaku). He later received Dharma transmission from the Chinese Ōbaku teacher Mu-an Hsing-tao.

The description Hakuin gives here of the elderly monk Jukaku, about whom nothing is known except that he was a former student of Tesshin whom Hakuin befriended at the temple, is quite different from the one in Tōrei's *Biography* (1713, Age 29), which portrays Jukaku as "looking half demented, with an unsightly face and a robe hanging in tatters from his body . . . he ran off when the master [Hakuin] tried to approach him."

8. Hakuin composed this verse upon suddenly penetrating the koan The Woman Comes Out of Dhyana (*Gateless Barrier*, case 42). (*Biography* [1713, Age 28]).

9. Not only did Hakuin, a Rinzai monk, seek out Sōtō and Ōbaku teachers during his travels, here he even depicts himself seriously considering an offer to become head priest at a Sōtō temple. This type of ecumenism seems to have been the rule in all three schools of Japanese Zen until well into the Meiji period, when sectarian barriers that new government policies had created began to stiffen.

10. Kogetsu Rōshi: Kogetsu Zenzai (also Zaikō, 1667–1751). Kogetsu taught at the Daikō-ji in Hyūga (present-day Miyazaki Prefecture), on the southernmost island of Kyushu. The Zen world of the time was said to be "divided between Kogetsu in the west and Hakuin in the east." Many of Hakuin's finest disciples, including Tōrei and Gasan Jitō (1727–1797), began their practice under Kogetsu. Tōrei's *Biography* says one of the main reasons Hakuin wanted to visit Kogetsu was because he had heard Kogetsu had attained an especially deep understanding of Ta-hui's verse on the lotus leaves (referred to several lines below), which Hakuin was struggling with at the time.

11. These are lines from a verse comment on the Mu koan by the Chinese master Ta-hui Tsung-kao (1089–1163), found in his discourses, *Ta-hui P'u-sho*, Chapter 3. The first two lines of the verse are: "The wind blows, willow flowers roll like balls; / The rain beats down, plum flowers flutter like butterflies."

12. For the events Hakuin alludes to here, see pp. 30–39. Hakuin refers frequently to this statement by the Sung master Ta-hui Tsung-kao that he had experienced "eighteen great satoris and countless

smaller ones." Although no source has been found for the statement among Ta-hui's voluminous records, Yoshizawa cites a reference in a work titled *Chu-ch'uang erh-pi* (*Jottings at the Bamboo Window, Second Series*), written by the noted Ming priest Yün-chi Chu-hung and published in the mid-seventeenth century (*Yasenkanna furoku*, p. 98).

13. In Tōrei's account in the *Biography* (1712, Age 27), Hakuin reconsiders his plan to travel to the island of Kyushu and visit Kogetsu because of far-fetched stories he overhears these monks relate about miraculous powers Kogetsu was said to possess. Tōrei (a former student of Kogetsu) comments that "Nothing the master heard from these monks would have enabled him to get a true picture of Kogetsu's Zen teaching, so he could only furrow his brow and think, 'If that's the kind of priest he is, there's nothing to be gained by visiting him.'"

14. Tetsudō Genchi (1658–1730) was the incumbent of the Enshō-ji, a Rinzai temple located in the hamlet of Ozaki near the city of Obama in Wakasa Province (present-day Fukui Prefecture). Tōrei's *Biography* places Hakuin's visit to Enshō-ji in 1713. Tetsudō is called Shōju's "Dharma uncle" because he was a brother monk of Shōju's teacher Shidō Munan. Sekiin Sōun (n.d.), a longtime student of Gudō Tōshoku (referred to here by his honorific title Hōkan Kokushi, National Master Hōkan) who served at the Heirin-ji in Musashi Province (present-day Saitama Prefecture), was known for his great severity in dealing with students.

15. In narrating his travels, Hakuin sometimes breaks into a parody of the poetical *michiyuki* style of composition common to a number of Japanese literary genres, in which the traveler, often a monk, describes the scenery and famous sites he passes, weaving the names of the places into the account, in a highly mannered style filled with poetic allusions and various kinds of wordplay. The two longest of these passages are distinguished by italic type.

16. To Hakuin's way of thinking, the words "great comfort and peace!" (*dai-anraku*) should properly issue only from someone who has actually experienced the tranquillity of great enlightenment by undergoing long years of post-satori training. Quite often in his writings, these words mark the speaker as a follower of quietist methods of Zen study such as the teaching of the Unborn, which enjoins people

not to introspect koans but to "remain just as they are in the Unborn Buddha-mind." Despite Hakuin's criticism of the practices he observed at Reishō-in (a Myōshin-ji temple in Mino Province, present-day Gifu Prefecture), he used the temple frequently as a stopover during his travels around central Japan. The head priest, unnamed here, was probably Bankyū Echō (d. 1719), a prominent Rinzai teacher who had studied under Bankei Yōtaku. According to Tōrei's *Biography* (1705, Age 20), Hakuin first visited Bankyū at the Reishō-in in 1705, at the beginning of his pilgrimage.

17. The Black-Rope Hell and Mountain-Crusher Hell are two of the Eight Great Hells.

18. Hakuin is declaring that he possesses the eye of enlightenment, which is said to be indestructible. The teachings of Unborn Zen, which enjoins students to "stay in the Unborn Buddha-mind" and not "to change it into anything else"—as, for example, by attempting to achieve enlightenment through rigorous austerities—are reflected in the priest's warnings about "unwanted meddling" or interference (*te-dashi*).

19. Tarumaru is probably Emon Sokai (n.d.), a Dharma heir of Bankei Yōtaku. According to Tōrei's *Biography*, Hakuin's first encounter with this priest, described as an exponent of "do-nothing" Zen, was in 1705, in his initial year of pilgrimage.

20. Musō Soseki (Musō Kokushi, 1275–1351), founder of the Tenryū-ji in Kyoto. Although Musō's religious biographies mention solitary retreats in this area of the country, I have been unable to find any other source for Tarumaru Sokai's story. Mount Kentoku is located in the north-central part of present-day Yamanashi Prefecture. An important temple, Kentoku-zan Erin-ji, was established at the site with Musō as its founder.

21. Jizō (Sanskrit, *Ksitigarbha*) is the Bodhisattva who appears in the world to assist sentient beings to salvation during the time between Shakyamuni's death and the appearance of Maitreya, the Buddha of the future. He is often depicted in the form of a young monk.

22. Mount Kokei (Kokei-zan: "Tiger Ravine Mountain") in Mino Province takes its name from an area of celebrated scenic beauty at Mount Lu in China. The Rinzai temple Eiho-ji (full name: Kokei-zan Eiho-ji) is located at Mount Kokei, having been built on the

site of a practice hermitage once used by Musō Sōseki. There is no mention in Hakuin's records that he visited the temple.

23. Ōta (part of the present-day city of Mino Kamo) was a post stop at an important river crossing on the Nakasendō road. According to the *Biography* (1715, Age 30), Hakuin visited the Manshaku-ji in 1715.

24. Chin Shuso (n.d.). Nothing is known of this monk.

25. According to Hakuin, Shōju used this saying to describe the difficulty Zen students had finding an authentic teacher. See Chapter 1, p. 32.

26. Mount Iwataki is located several kilometers north of Ōta, not far from the mountains of Ibuka where, four hundred years earlier, the greatly revered Kanzan Egen, founder of the Myōshin-ji, had secluded himself to engage in solitary practice. According to Katō Shōshun, the rundown hut that Layman Shikano restored for Hakuin had originally stood within the precincts of a small temple named Jingō-ji. *Hakuin Oshō Nempu*, p. 150. A brief sketch of Layman Tokugen (Shikano Yoshibei, n.d.) and account of the hut is included in *Poison Stamens in a Thicket of Thorns*, 5 (*Hakuin Oshō Zenshū* 2, p. 131).

Chapter 3

1. Tōrei's *Biography* (1715, Age 30) describes an encounter Hakuin had at about this time with a demonic apparition it describes as the god of the mountain:

> The master was sitting late into the night. Around about midnight, he heard the crunch of feet on the ground outside the hut. There was a creak as of a door opening, and someone entered the hut. He was huge, standing eight or nine feet in height, with the rough appearance of a *yamabushi* or mountain ascetic. A loud voice boomed out, "Master Ekaku!" But the master did not look around or make any reply. After what seemed a long time, the figure disappeared. When the master got up and surveyed the room, he found the door still bolted securely; there was no sign that anyone had entered. The master then realized the visitor who had come to test his mettle was no ordinary being.

2. The story of Musō Kokushi's solitary retreat appeared at the end of the previous chapter.

3. Hakuin suggests that the practice of zazen, or seated meditation, should lead to a satori so powerful as to be accompanied, as it was in his case, by an experience of overwhelming joy. See the appendix: "Preface to *Idle Talk on a Night Boat*." p. 122.

4. National Master Gudō (Gudō Tōshoku, 1577–1661), the master of Shidō Munan, Shōju Rōjin's teacher, was in Hakuin's eyes an important link in the Myōshin-ji transmission, having kept the authentic traditions of the school alive at a crucial time during the seventeenth century. When the Ming priest Yin-yüan Lung-ch'i arrived in Japan with a large contingent of monks and a syncretic form of Ming Buddhism, and certain Myōshin-ji clerics considered offering him the abbotship of the monastery, Gudō refused to allow it. In 1758, at the age of seventy-four, Hakuin wrote a work titled *Lingering Light from Precious Mirror*, expressly to clarify Gudō's importance and the contribution he had made to Japanese Zen.

   As usual, Hakuin lumps into the "silent illumination" category all students who do not make the breakthrough into kenshō the central concern of their religious practice.

5. The expression "covered bowls of plain unvarnished wood" (*shiraki gōshi*) is descriptive of something in its original, unvarnished purity. Here the priests refer to a state of mind prior to the arising of discriminations such as might occur in attempting to solve koans through intellectual means. Their comments throughout this paragraph are reminiscent of Zen master Bankei's expositions of his teaching of the Unborn. See *Unborn: The Life and Teaching of Zen Master Bankei*.

6. See Chapter 1, note 68.

7. The story of the priest called Sanuki (or Sanukibō) that Hakuin gives below is found in Mujū Ichien's *Gathering of Sand and Pebbles* (*Shaseki-shū*), *kan* 2. Hakuin takes up the story in considerable detail in his work *Lingering Light from Precious Mirror* (*Hōkan Ishō*), *Hakuin Oshō Zenshū* 1, pp. 252–4):

> The priest Ronshikibō spent his religious life living in a small hermitage in the mountains of Ikoma near Osaka, devoting himself to the constant recitation of the *Lotus Sutra*. When he died, he left the hermitage to his disciple Sanukibō, a follower of the doctrine that all things end with death, a teaching that denies the Buddhist principle of karmic cause and

effect. Sanukibō survived his teacher by four or five years; when he died, he fell directly into the evil realms. Once there, he saw in a small hermitage very much like his own at Ikoma the figure of his former teacher Ronshikibō, reciting the *Lotus Sutra*. Sanukibō could not understand how a priest who had led such an exemplary life could suffer such an ignominious rebirth. He learned from Ronshikibō that he had undergone this retribution because he had lacked the Mind of Enlightenment: all his recitations of the *Lotus Sutra* had been done for his own benefit alone—a practice of the Lesser Vehicle—and he had not had any concern for the suffering of others. Now he constantly lamented his condition and the inadequacy of his religious resolve, which he brought on himself by thinking only of his own salvation.

8. A doctrine that teaches that all things end with death would, by denying the principle of transmigratory rebirth, be un-Buddhist.

   There is a story similar to this one about a woman who cheated customers by using a false measure in Suzuki Shōsan's *Tales of Cause and Effect*.

9. This priest is probably Daikyū Ebō, 1715–1774, a disciple of Hakuin, who conducted a very large lecture-meeting on the *Record of Wu-chun* at the Tōfuku-ji in Kyoto in 1764. *Tōfukuji-shi* (*Annals of the Tōfuku-ji*), Shiraishi Hōryū, 1930.

10. In the *Suiriku* ceremony (*Suiriku-e*: another name for *Segaki-e*), food and drink are offered for the liberation of all beings of water (*sui*) and land (*riku*).

11. It seems that Hakuin was the object of some criticism in certain Zen circles. His student Genshoku alludes to it in his preface to *Talks Introductory to Lectures on the Record of Hsi-keng* (*The Essential Teachings of Zen Master Hakuin*, p. 1), where he attributes the criticism to priests who were jealous of Hakuin's success.

12. Hakuin used this verse by Gudō Tōshoku as an inscription on a number of "portraits" he painted of Gudō; they consist of a single large Chinese character for *Gu* ("Ignorant"—the first of the two characters in Gudō's name, *see* illus., p. 71) written in a highly cursive style that makes it resemble the abbreviated one- or two-stroke paintings of Bodhidharma found in Zen-style painting. Gudō is said to have inscribed the verse in response to one that his student Emperor Go-Mizunoo had written above a portrait of Gudō he

had drawn, also consisting of the single character *Gu* (Takeuchi, *Hakuin*, plate 42).

13. Chang Liang and Ch'en P'ing are great heroes of ancient China.

14. P'eng Tsu is the Chinese Methuselah. The First Principle (*Dai-ichigi*) is explained as the supreme truth, nonobjectifiable and un-transmittable, which is transmitted from master to disciple in the Zen tradition.

15. The Wild Ivy deity (*Itsumadegusa myōjin*). The name was probably invented by Hakuin. See the introduction, p. xli.

16. This saying of the Yuan priest Kao-feng Yüan-miao (1238–1295) contains perhaps Hakuin's favorite formulation of the requisites for Zen study. Originally from *Kao-feng's Zen Essentials* (*Kao-feng ho-shang ch'an-yao*), it also appears in *Son-ga kyui-gam* (Japanese, *Zenke-kikan*), a Korean Zen work that was widely read in Japanese Zen circles.

17. A saying from the *Nirvana Sutra*.

18. For the earlier reference to "meddling and interference," see Chapter 2, note 18.

19. Aniruddha, who was a cousin as well as a disciple of the Buddha, was once severely admonished by the Buddha when he fell asleep while listening to him preach a sermon. He thereupon vowed never to sleep again, as a consequence of which he eventually went blind but later developed extraordinary powers of perception (*Lotus Sutra*, Chapter 8).

20. These are all koans of the *nantō*, or "difficult-to-pass," type.

21. Yōzan Keiyō (1559–1626), of the important Shōtaku-in subtemple of the Myōshin-ji, was the teacher of Gudō Tōshoku.

22. The Shōden-ji and Daisen-ji are in Mino Province, present-day Gifu Prefecture.

23. Shidō Munan Anju (1603–1676); *Anju* means "Master of the Hermitage." Like Hakuin, Munan was the son of an innkeeper. The family inn was of the *honjin*-type used by daimyos, located on the Tōkaidō at the Sekigahara post station in Mino Province. Being kept by his family responsibilities from carrying out his desire to enter the priesthood, Munan studied for many years as a layman, receiving instruction from Gudō Tōshoku when the latter stopped at Munan's inn on his travels between Kyoto and Edo. Finally, at the age of fifty-one, Munan accompanied Gudō to Edo and re-

ceived his permission to take religious vows. He spent the rest of his life in Edo, living at the Shidō-an hermitage, refusing all offers to serve at large and important temples, and focusing his teaching effort toward the lay community. For a translation of Tōrei's *Biography of Zen Master Shidō Munan*, see *Eastern Buddhist* 3, no. 1 (1970), pp. 124–38.

24. Dōkyō Etan Rōkan: Shōju Rōjin; *Rōkan* means "Old Man." Tetsuzui Genshō (1640–1745) and Chōmon Zen'a (1661–1714) are not mentioned among Munan's heirs in Tōrei's *Biography of Zen Master Shidō Munan*. Sumpu is the modern city of Shizuoka.

25. Tz'u-ming (Shih-shuang Ch'u-yüan). See Chapter 1, note 42.

26. Shūhō Myōchō (1282–1338), the deeply revered founder of the Daitoku-ji in Kyoto; better known by the honorific title Daitō Kokushi. Hakuin also refers to him as Myōchō Daishi, or Great Teacher Myōchō. Daitō's dedication to religious practice is legendary: one story, current from about the fifteenth century, tells of "twenty years of silence" following Daitō's enlightenment when he lived with beggars under the Gojō Bridge in Kyoto. Another describes him seating himself on his meditation seat just before his death and breaking his crippled leg with his own strength so he could die in a proper full lotus posture (Miura and Sasaki, *Zen Dust*, pp. 233–34). The provenance of the story Hakuin tells here is unknown.

27. The source of this verse is unknown; it is not included in *Ox-Herding Poems for Leisurely Humming* (*Yōgyū-keigin ka*), the collection of didactic religious waka (*dōka*) published under Daitō's name in the seventeenth century.

28. Tetsuzui Genshō. See Chapter 3, note 24.

29. Chōmon Zen'a. See Chapter 3, note 24.

30. The *sanri* and *kyokuchi* are points on the body where moxa punk is placed and burned in moxabustion therapy. The *sanri* is just below the outer base of the kneecap; the *kyokuchi*, near the lateral crease of the elbow.

31. See Chapter 1, note 77.

32. The verse is attributed to Musō Soseki (*Oniazami furoku*, p. 16).

33. At some point after the death of Hakuin's mother, the Shōin-ji became the Nagasawas' family temple (*bodai-ji*). The priest Tanrei Soden, who died shortly after ordaining Hakuin, was succeeded at Shōin-ji by Tōrin Soshō (d. 1754), a monk who had formerly studied

with Hakuin's teacher Sokudō Fueki at the Daishō-ji. The Shōin-ji was vacant at this time because Tōrin, who suffered from chronic ill health and was perhaps no longer willing to brave the privations at the poverty-stricken temple, had left (fled?). It is puzzling that Hakuin here links his "late master" to the Shōin-ji, since the person he apparently regarded as his master, Sokudō Fueki, never resided at Shōin-ji. The Shōin-ji priest immediately prior to Hakuin must have been Tōrin Soshō, who is nowhere mentioned as Hakuin's teacher.

34. Nothing else is known of the elderly servant Yake (referred to in some sources as Yobakari and Yoke) Shichibei. Hakuin's father is referred to by his posthumous religious name, Heishin Sōi.

35. Daizui Rōjin: Daizui Sōiku (d. 1660), who had studied as a young monk at the Daishō-ji in Numazu, was the restorer of the Shōin-ji. As a young boy, Hakuin's father, a nephew of Daizui, had studied under him at Shōin-ji.

36. The Confucian *Analects*.

37. Hakuin uses the term *Introspective Meditation* (*Naikan;* the subject of Chapter 4 of *Wild Ivy*) to describe meditative techniques performed mainly for therapeutic purposes. In *Idle Talk on a Night Boat* (virtually the same text as Chapter 4), a number of techniques are set forth for concentrating the *ki* energy in the lower body, including the so-called soft-butter (*nanso*) method, which are said to cure illness and sustain physical health. In the preface to *Idle Talk on a Night Boat* (see the appendix), Hakuin also uses the term *Introspective Meditation* to describe a method of meditation that involves the introspection of koan-like statements. Apparently, this meditation, which has been called "horizontal zazen," was devised by Hakuin himself, a result of his attempts to integrate therapeutic *Naikan* techniques with Zen-type meditation. Several times, he states that he had succeeded in working out such a method of meditation as he was striving to cure himself of Zen sickness by practicing the *Naikan* techniques he had learned from Master Hakuyū.

38. Shōtō Rōkan, "Old Man Shōtō," has not been identified. This was perhaps a popular saying of the time; a similar phrase with slightly different wording is found in the *Blue Cliff Record,* case 83.

39. The *Blue Cliff Record* (*Pi-yen lu;* the principal koan collection used in the Rinzai school); *Record of Hsü-t'ang* (Zen records of the Sung

master Hsü-t'ang Chih-yü); *Praise of the True School* (*Wu-chia cheng-tsung tsan*); *Three Teachings of the Buddha Patriarchs* (*Fo-tsu san-ching*); *Record of Lin-chi* (Zen records of T'ang master Lin-chi I-hsüan); *Ta-hui's Letters* (*Ta-hui shu;* letters of religious instruction by the Sung master Ta-hui Tsung-kao); *Records of Daitō, Fa-yen, Sung-yüan,* and *Bukkō* (Zen records of Daitō Kokushi, the Sung masters Wu-tsu Fa-yen and Sung-yüan Ch'ung-yueh, and Bukkō Kokushi—the National Master title of the Sung priest Wu-hsüeh Tsu-yüan, who taught in Kamakura, Japan, and whose Zen records were published there); *Tsung-ying Verse Collection* (*Tsung-ying chi,* a collection of religious verse by Hsüeh-tou Ch'ung-hsien); *Poems of Cold Mountain* (*Han-shan shih*); *Spurring Students through the Zen Barrier* (*Ch'an-kuan ts'e-chin*); *Four-Part Collection* (*Shibu-roku,* a Japanese collection comprising the Zen poems *Hsin-hsin-ming* and *Cheng-tao-ko;* the *Ten Ox-Herding Pictures;* and the *Ts'o-ch'an-i,* or *Principles of Zazen*); *Ta-hui's Arsenal* (*Ta-hui wu-k'u*). There is no *Manjushri's Held-in-Hand Sutra* (*Monju Shunai Kyō*); it may refer to the *Heart Sutra,* a text not included in this list of works but one Hakuin is known to have lectured on more than once. Since the *Heart Sutra* is a wisdom-class sutra and Manjushri the personification of wisdom, it is possible that Hakuin coined this title to underscore that his Zen lectures are not mere elucidations of text but utterances of religious truth proceeding directly from the wisdom source he "holds in his hand." The *Precious Mirror Samadhi* (*Pao-ching san-mei*) is a Zen verse; *Dream Words from the Land of Dreams* (*Kaian Kokugo*) is Hakuin's chief work in the traditional Zen commentarial genre; *Poison Stamens in a Thicket of Thorns* (*Keisō Dokuzui*) contains Hakuin's Zen records; *Record of Daiō* (Zen records of Daiō Kokushi: Nampo Jōmyō); *Song of the Mind-King* (*Hsin-wang mei*).

40. The Japanese titles of the works given here: *Poison Stamens in a Thicket of Thorns: Keisō Dokuzui. Lingering Light from Precious Mirror: Hōkan Ishō* ("Precious Mirror," Hōkan, is Gudō Tōshoku, from his posthumous title Hōkan Kokushi). *Idle Talk on a Night Boat: Yasenkanna. My Teakettle: Orategama* (a collection of Hakuin's religious letters). *A Weed-Choked Field of Words: Kana Mugura* (made up of two works: *Shin Dangi* [*New Preaching*] and *Tsuji Dangi* [*Preaching at the Crossroads*]). *Goose Grass: Yaemugura* (made up of

A *Record of Four Filial Daughters, A Record of Miraculous Effects Achieved by the Ten-Phrase Kannon Sutra*, and, in one rare edition, *Childhood Tales*). *Tea-Grinding Song* (two such songs exist: *Otafuku-jorō Kohiki Uta* [*Tea-Grinding Song of the Ugly Prostitute*] and *Shushin Obaba Kohiki Uta* [*Grain-Grinding Song of the Old Woman Mind-as-Master*]). *A Record of Four Filial Young Girls: Takazuka Shijō Kōki. Childhood Tales: Osana Monogatari* (an autobiography paralleling much of the material in *Wild Ivy*, included as a third *kan* in some editions of *Goose Grass*). *Yūkichi's Tale: Yūkichi Monogatari* (printed in a postscript to the third *kan* in a rare edition of *Goose Grass*). *Dream Words from the Land of Dreams: Kaian Kokugo* (Hakuin's chief work in the traditional Zen commentarial style, patterned on the *Blue Cliff Record*). *Usenshikō* (the meaning of the title is uncertain). *An Application of Moxa: Sashimogusa* (the meaning of this title is also uncertain). *Snake Strawberries: Hebiichigo. A Record of Sendai's Comments on the Cold Mountain Poems: Kanzan-shi Sendai-kimon* (a Zen commentary on the poems of Han-shan). *Horse Thistles: Oniazami. Dharma Talks Introductory to Lectures on the Record of Hsi-keng: Sokkō-roku Kaien-fusetsu. Wild Ivy: Itsumadegusa*. For more bibliographical information, see *Zen Master Hakuin: Selected Writings*, pp. 223–33.

41. Hakuin's answer to this question is given in Chapter 4 of *Wild Ivy*. See Chapter 4, note 3.

Chapter 4

As mentioned earlier, the text of Chapter 4 is almost identical to the work known as *Idle Talk on a Night Boat* (Japanese, *Yasenkanna*), in which Hakuin describes the "Zen sickness" he contracted in his latter twenties and the methods he learned from the recluse Hakuyū in the mountains outside Kyoto that enabled him to cure the ailment. The story of his visit to Master Hakuyū first appeared as an extensive note in *A Record of Sendai's Comments on the Cold Mountain Poems* (*Kanzan-shi Sendai-kimon*), Hakuin's commentary on the poems of Han-shan, or Cold Mountain, published in 1746. When *Idle Talk on a Night Boat*, the best-known version of the story, appeared eleven years later, in 1757, the text had grown in total wordage by about one-fourth. Here, in adapting

Idle Talk on a Night Boat for inclusion in *Wild Ivy*, Hakuin transformed the original Japanese prose into Chinese verse so it would conform to the rest of the text. He also omitted the long preface that had accompanied *Idle Talk*, made some minor additions to the text, and added some paragraphs at the beginning to smooth the transition from the previous chapter and several pages at the end, which include up-to-date information about Hakuyū. The *Wild Ivy* text is thus the longest and most complete version of the Hakuyū story.

Idle Talk on a Night Boat, which has always been the most popular of Hakuin's writings, seems to have been in print almost constantly since it was published in the eighteenth century. Doubts long raised about the historicity of the two- or three-hundred-year-old cave-dwelling Hakuyū, whom many had regarded as a product of Hakuin's fertile imagination, were laid to final rest in the 1960s by researchers who established that a man using the sobriquet Hakuyū did in fact exist at about this time. His real name was Ishikawa Jishun (1645–1709), and he was probably a student of the samurai turned recluse Ishikawa Jōzan (1583–1672), whose well-known villa Shisendō was located in the Shirakawa District of eastern Kyoto. In 1661, at the age of fifteen, Jishun entered the hills in back of the Shisendō and took up residence in a cave. He was visited there in 1692 by the Neo-Confucian teacher Kaibara Ekken (1630–1714). He remained in his cave, shunning the world, until 1709, forty-eight years later, when he died from injuries incurred in a fall from a cliff.

With the confirmation of Hakuyū's existence, the question then became whether Hakuin had actually visited him or whether he had made the story up. I don't think anyone is likely to come up with any evidence that will prove the matter incontrovertibly one way or the other. However, those who have studied most closely what is an extremely complicated issue seem to agree that Hakuin did not visit Hakuyū but was merely using the colorful figure of the old hermit to dramatize certain methods of meditation he had worked out on his own and found to be effective for preserving health and curing illnesses common among monks engaged in the rigors of Zen training.

One of the most persuasive reasons cited for the tale's being fiction is Hakuin's choice of a title. *Idle Talk on a Night Boat* derives from a popular saying—"night boat on the Shirakawa River" (*Shirakawa yobune* or *yasen*)—which is based on the story of a countryman who brags to his friends that he has been to Kyoto and seen its marvelous sights. When asked about the Shirakawa River (the site of Hakuyū's cave and in fact a shallow stream), he bluffed and replied that he couldn't rightly describe it because it was nighttime when his boat floated by. In calling his story *Idle Talk on a Night Boat*, then, Hakuin was most probably alerting readers at the outset that he was only pretending he had been to see Hakuyū and was engaging in fiction.

In any event, it is clear that Hakuin wrote the work primarily to offer monks engaged in Zen training a means of maintaining health and to give those already suffering from Zen sickness a recipe for curing themselves. In the late work *Horse Thistles*, he describes a vow he took during his own battle against Zen sickness:

> I pledged that if I did free myself from the pit of falsehood into which I had fallen and went on to achieve a genuine enlightenment, I would do everything in my power to assist others who might suffer from Zen sickness as I had. In time, I met a wise man [Hakuyū] . . . whose teaching gradually enabled me to eradicate my illness to its very roots. Now . . . whenever I see signs of Zen sickness developing in younger students, I get the same feeling I would have if I saw a small infant toddling toward an open well.

1. In *Idle Talk on a Night Boat,* appears a similar paragraph in the preface (see appendix); here Hakuin inserts it at the beginning of the text. Neither of the two men mentioned here (they also appear later in the text) has been identified. In fact, in the course of his writings, Hakuin attributes this same quotation to at least five different people, so it seems likely that he either wrote it himself or cobbled it together from various Taoist texts. He used it frequently for calligraphic inscriptions. *See* illus., p. 88.

2. *Vital energy* translates the term *ki* (Chinese, *ch'i*), a key concept in traditional Chinese thought and medical theory. It has been rendered into English in various ways—for example, vital energy, primal energy, breath, vital breath, spirit. *Ki*-energy, circulating through the human body, is vital to the preservation of health and sustenance of life and plays a prominent part in the methods of Introspective Meditation that Hakuin learned from Master Hakuyū. The "external" alchemy of the Taoist tradition involved the search for a "pill" or "elixir" of immortality, the most important

element of which was a mercury compound (cinnabar). Once found and taken into the body, it was supposed to assure immortality and ascent to heaven, commonly on the back of a crane.

Hakuyū's instruction is concerned rather with the internal ramifications of this tradition, in which the "elixir" is cultivated in the area of the lower *tanden*, the "elixir field" or "cinnabar field," also called the *kikai tanden*, "the ocean of *ki*-energy," the center of breathing or center of strength, located slightly below the navel. Hakuin describes the terms in *Orategama*: "Although the *tanden* is located in three places in the body, the one to which I refer is the lower *tanden*. The *kikai* and the *tanden*, which are virtually identical, are both located below the navel. The *tanden* is two inches below the navel, the *kikai* an inch and a half below it. It is in this area that the true *ki*-energy always accumulates."

3. This is the layman who appeared at the end of Chapter 3 and asked Hakuin to explain more fully a reference he had made to Introspective Meditation (Japanese, *Naikan*). Hakuin's answer becomes the subject of Chapter 4. Although the word *Naikan*, which appears in earlier Chinese Buddhism (for example, Chih-i's *Great Concentration and Insight*, Chapter 5) to indicate a type of meditation directed within oneself, is generally used by Hakuin for contemplations performed specifically for therapeutic benefit (for instance, the "butter method" he learned from Hakuyū), he also seems to use it for a more Zen-type introspection using koan-like themes. See Chapter 3, note 37.

4. A reference to a well-known saying from *The Doctrine of the Mean*.

5. This was a basic notion in Chinese medical lore. Cf. the statement in the encyclopedic compilation *Wu tsa tsu* (*Five Assorted Offerings*, the section on "Man"), by the Ming scholar Hsieh Chao-che: "When a person is engaged in too much intellection, the heart fire burns excessively and mounts upward." Tōrei's *Biography* (1710, Age 25) lists twelve morbid symptoms that appeared: firelike burning in the head; loins and legs ice-cold; eyes constantly watering; ringing in the ears; instinctive shrinking from sunlight; irrepressible sadness in darkness or shade; thinking an intolerable burden; recurrent bad dreams sapping his strength; emission of semen during sleep; restlessness and nervousness during waking hours; difficulty digesting food; cold chills unrelieved by heavy clothing.

6. The samurai Ishikawa Jōzan (1583–1672) retired to the hills northeast of Kyoto in 1641. His residence, the Shisendō (Hall of Poetry Immortals), is located on a hillside overlooking the northern part of Kyoto. See Thomas Rimer, *Shisendō* (New York: Weatherhill, 1991). There are several caves Hakuyū is said to have inhabited located in the hills behind the Shisendō.

7. Hakuin was twenty-five in 1710. According to the chronology he gives in Chapter 3 of *Wild Ivy*, however, he visited Hakuyū just prior to his return to Shōin-ji, in or about his thirty-first year (see the prefatory remarks to the notes to Chapter 4). In *Idle Talk on a Night Boat*, Hakuin states that Hakuyū was between one hundred and eighty and two hundred and forty years old and gives the distance of his cave from other human habitation as three to four leagues.

8. The three books are intended to show Hakuyū's roots in the three traditions: Confucianism, Taoism, and Buddhism.

9. P'ien Ch'iao, Ts'ang Kung, and Hua T'o are three celebrated physicians of ancient China.

10. An adage, originally from the *Ju Ta-ch'eng lun*, that also appears in *The Records of the Lamp of the Ching-te Era* (*Ching-te ch'uan-teng lu*), Chapter 1, the section on Upagupta.

11. In *A Record of Sendai's Comments on the Cold Mountain Poems*, the earliest version of the story, Hakuin at this point has Hakuyū say: "You must be careful you do not divulge the secret method recklessly to others. If you do, not only will it hurt you, it will be very harmful to me as well."

12. Traditional Chinese medical theory describes the *ki*-energy as moving constantly between the five internal organs: lungs, heart, spleen, liver, kidneys. If they do not maintain a full and vital supply of *ki*-energy, or if the *ki*-energy becomes stagnant, illness results. "Defensive energy" is a form of *ki*-energy that protects the surface of the body against external pathogenic factors. "Nutritive blood" (or "nourishing *ki*"—blood was thought to circulate together with *ki*-energy) is *ki*-energy, produced from food, that flows through the blood vessels, circulating through the body and supplying it with nutrients.

13. In traditional Chinese medical theory, the concepts of wood, fire, earth, metal, and water (the five "phases": *wu-hsing*) are used to

define qualities of energy within the body in a process of mutual production and mutual overcoming. They serve as the core for a system of relations and correspondences that, together with the yin-yang theory, operate in cycles of rise and fall and in a universal pattern, uniting humans and nature. The five phases are tied to many corresponding categories of five—among them, the five internal organs (lungs, heart, liver, spleen, and kidneys), corresponding to metal, fire, wood, earth, and water, respectively. Maintaining the correct balance between them is essential for preserving health.

The internal organs are regarded as having seven marvelous powers: liver, the aspect of the soul (*hun*) belonging to heaven; lungs, the aspect of the soul (*p'o*) belonging to earth; heart, the spirit; spleen, thought and knowledge; kidneys, life essence and will.

14. The six viscera or "treasuries" are the large intestine, small intestine, gallbladder, stomach, urinary bladder, and the *san chiao,* or "triple heater," which is described as a network of energetic conduits that participate in the metabolic functions located in three parts of the body cavity: one below the heart and above the stomach, another in the stomach area, and a third above the urinary bladder.

15. The seven "misfortunes"—joy, anger, grief, pleasure, love, hate, and desire—are so called because they are the causes of illness.

16. The four evils are harmful influences to the body caused by wind, cold, heat, and moisture.

17. There are various explanations offered for these categories, none of them altogether convincing. I have rendered them tentatively as the *five senses* (the five organs of sense: eyes, ears, nose, tongue, and skin) and *six roots* (the first four of the five senses plus the tactile body and the mind). *Left side* and *right side* are said to indicate areas on the wrists where the pulses from the five internal organs appear.

18. Some commentators identify Hsü Chun as the Korean physician Hŏ Chun (n.d.), although the quotation has not been found among his works. The "lower heater" and "upper heater" are two elements of the *san chiao,* or "triple heater," described above (Chapter 4, note 14). In all these quotations, the essential point is keeping the vital energy in the lower body.

19. This is a sobriquet of the Yuan physician Ch'en Chih-hsü, who is described as an adept in the Taoist arts of prolonging life. The source of the quotation is unknown. Here and in the following sec-

tion, various permutations of the divination signs in the *Book of Changes* are used in describing the movement of vital energy within the body. The *Book of Changes* (*I Ching*), one of the five classics of Confucianism, is a manual on divination used since ancient times. It is based on five diagrams made up of trigrams, three lines, undivided and divided, which are increased by doubling them into hexagrams to sixty-four. Attached to each hexagram is a short and highly enigmatic essay ascribing a meaning to each line of the hexagram.

20. The "twelve conduits": there is a conduit for each of the five internal organs and six viscera and one additional conduit for the heart, lungs, and aorta.

21. *The Treatise on Prolonging Life* (*Enju-sho*): there are several Chinese and Japanese works with similar titles; the quotation itself has not been traced.

22. These are the same two gentlemen who appeared at the beginning of the chapter.

23. A dialogue between Kuang Ch'eng and the Yellow Emperor (Huang Ti) is found in the *Chuang Tzu*. See *Chuang Tzu*, translated by Burton Watson (New York: Columbia University Press, 1968), pp. 118–20.

24. The state of five nonleakages (*go-muro*) is attained when afflicting passions disappear from the mind. In *Orategama*, Hakuin has Hakuyū say that when this state—in which eyes, ears, tongue, body, and mind all function without illusion—is achieved, the *ki*-energy will accumulate before your eyes.

25. Neither the identity of this person nor the source of the quotation has been identified.

26. Mencius explains this "vast, expansive energy" (*hao jan chih ch'i*) as "immense and flood-like, unyielding in the highest degree. If man nourishes it with integrity and places no obstacle in its path, it will fill all Heaven and Earth and he will be in the same stream as Heaven itself" (D. C. Lau, *Mencius* [New York: Penguin, 1970] Book II, part a.2).

27. In other words, when this threshold (described here as a kind of satori) is achieved, you realize that the Great Way and the elixir are one.

28. In *Preaching at the Crossroads* (*Tsuji-dangi*), Hakuin explains

"churning the long river into the finest butter" as the activity of the enlightened person working to assist other beings to enlightenment.

29. The source of this quotation has not been identified.

30. Li Shih-ts'ai was a noted Ming dynasty physician who wrote several important medical works.

31. "After Completion" and "Before Completion" are the two final hexagrams in the *Book of Changes*.

32. Tan-hsi is the sobriquet of the Yuan dynasty physician Chu Chen-heng. Here it refers to the school of medicine he founded.

33. These are the three worlds (the world of desire, the world of form, and the world of formlessness) in which sentient beings transmigrate.

34. "Diverse contemplation" (*ta-kan*) presumably refers to unfocused koan-type meditation in which the meditation topic becomes the object of discrimination and *ki*-energy fails to gather in the lower body. "Noncontemplation" (*mu-kan*) would then be an ultimate meditational state in which all intellectual discrimination is cut off.

35. Although no source has been found for the words that Hakuin here attributes to the Buddha, a similar teaching is found in Chih-i's *Great Concentration and Insight*.
Agama sutras: a generic term for all Hinayana sutras.

36. *The Great Concentration and Insight* (*Mo-ho chih-kuan*), one of the major works of the T'ien-t'ai teacher Chih-i (538–597), is a manual of religious practice in twenty *chüan*. The eighth *chüan* is devoted to therapeutic-type meditation.

37. These two concentrations, achieved during samadhi and leading to clear discernment, appear in Chih-i's *Great Concentration and Insight*. In the concentration on ultimate truth (*taishin-shi*), one realizes that illusion is, as such, true reality. In the concentration on temporary truth (*ken'en-shi*), the mind ceases to be affected by changing conditions within and without.

38. T'ien-t'ung Ju-ching (1163–1228), the Sung dynasty Ts'ao-t'ung (Japanese Sōtō) Zen master best known as the teacher of Dōgen Kigen (1200–1252), founder of the Japanese Sōtō school. The teaching is found in Dōgen's practice diary *Hōkyō-ki*, which he kept while he was studying Zen in China. See Norman Waddell, "Dōgen's *Hōkyō-ki*," part 2, *Eastern Buddhist* 11, no. 1 (1977), p. 81.

39. *The Smaller Concentration and Insight* (*Hsiao chih-kuan*) is an

abridgment of *The Great Concentration and Insight*, which Chih-i is said to have compiled for his sick brother. The story, according to *Yasenkanna Hyōshaku* (p. 114), appears in an appendix to *The Smaller Concentration and Insight*. It is also found in the *Fo-tsu t'ung-chi*, *chüan* 10.

40. The source of this quotation has not been traced. The name *Po-yün* (Japanese, *Hakuun*) is common to a great many Chinese and Japanese priests. In another work, Hakuin attributes the quotation to the Sung priest Huang-lung Hui-nan. *Hakuin Oshō Zenshū*, 6; p. 445.

41. *Su Wen* (*Plain Questions*) is the title of the first part of the ancient Chinese medical treatise *Huang Ti Nei-ching* (*The Yellow Emperor's Manual of Corporeal Medicine*), the basic medical text in Tokugawa Japan.

42. P'eng Tsu is the Chinese Methuselah. Yoshizawa has found a passage similar in content to this one in a work by Su Tung-p'o, who ascribes it to the T'ang recluse Sun Ssu-miao (d. 682), the author of several Taoist medical treatises. *Yasenkanna furoku*, p. 76.

43. The celebrated poet and Zen layman Su Tung-p'o (1037–1110) was deeply versed in Taoist medical techniques and wrote several works on the subject. The quotation has not been found among his writings. *Yasenkanna furoku*, p. 78.

44. Yoshizawa gives Ch'u Ch'eng's *Ch'u-shih i-shu* as a source for this saying. *Yasenkanna furoku*, p. 81.

45. A "soft-butter method" (*nanso no hō*) of meditation somewhat similar to the one described below has been found among the Agama sutras (Itō Kazuyoshi, *Hakuyūshi shijitsu no shinkenkyu* [Kyoto: Yamaguchi Shoten, 1960], pp. 65–66).

46. A young man named Lu-sheng on his way to seek a career in the capital stopped off at a place called Han-tan. While waiting for his lunch to cook, he took a nap and dreamed that he rose through the ranks and finally attained the post of prime minister. When he woke and saw his food still cooking on the fire, he realized that life is an empty dream and returned to his home.

47. Here Rikugawa Taiun quotes a comment by Reigen Etō, a student of Hakuin who became one of his chief heirs: "When he was young, the master [Hakuin] wore three layers of heavy-soled *tabi* on his feet. [Later,] after he learned to bring his mind down into his 'cin-

nabar field (*tanden*),' he never even went near a brazier, even during the coldest part of the winter" *Yasenkanna Hyōshaku* (Tokyo: Sankibō, 1982) p. 193.

48. Most of the text in this final section was added by Hakuin at the time he wrote *Wild Ivy*; it is not found in *Idle Talk on a Night Boat*.

49. These lines are from a poem by the Sung dynasty poet and Zen layman Huang Ting-chien (1045–1115). *Yasenkanna Hyōshaku* (p. 146) offers the following explanation: When you are busily engaged in some activity, you won't even notice the sound of a horse munching its fodder, but that same noise can be very distracting when you are trying to take a nap. Hence, even this poor story I have written about Introspective Meditation may, given the right conditions, receive people's attention.

Appendix

1. The attribution "Compiled by Hunger and Cold, the Master of Poverty Hermitage" was used by Hakuin in other of his works. The preface is written by Hakuin himself.

2. Sung Yü and Ho Yen were celebrated for their fine masculine beauty. The lives of renowned poets Tu Fu and Chia Tao were characterized by periods of extreme privation. The poet Ch'ü Yüan committed suicide by throwing himself into the Mi-lo River after being subjected to unjust slander.

3. Hua T'o is a legendary Chinese physician.

4. These lines from a verse by the T'ang poet Ya Tang appear in the *San-t'i shih* (Japanese, *San-tai shi*), a collection of T'ang poetry that was much read and studied in Japanese Zen circles.

BIBLIOGRAPHY

Works in Japanese

Abe Hōshun. *Shōju Rōjin.* Tokyo: 1931.

Akiyama Kanji. *Shamon Hakuin.* Privately printed. Shizuoka: 1983.

Biography of Zen Priest Hakuin (*see* Tōrei Enji). Page numbers refer to Katō Shōshun's *Hakuin Oshō Nempu.*

Fukuba Hōshū. *Hakuin.* Tokyo: 1941.

Hakuin Ekaku. *Itsumadegusa* (*Wild Ivy*). Shidō-an: Shōin-ji, 1768.

"Hakuin Kenkyū." Special issue of the journal *Zendō* (Tokyo, 1918).

Hakuin Zenji Nempu (*Chronological Biography of Zen Master Hakuin*). Mishima: Ryūtaku-ji, 1967.

Hakuin Zenji Shū (*Collection of Zen Master Hakuin's Writings*). Edited by Tokiwa Daijō. Dainihonbunko: bukkyō-hen no. 13. Tokyo: 1938.

Hakuin Oshō Zenshū (*Complete Works of Zen Priest Hakuin*). Tokyo: 1935, 8 vols.

Hakuin Zenji Jihitsu Kokuhon Shūsei (*A Collection of Woodblock-Printed Reproductions of Zen Master Hakuin's Facsimile Holograph Editions*). Edited by Yoshizawa Katsuhiro. Kyoto: 1996.

Itō Kazuō. *Hakuyūshi.* Kyoto: Yamaguchi Shoten, 1973.

Oniazami furoku (supplement to *Oniazami*). Annotated edition of *Horse Thistles* in *Hakuin Zenji Jihitsu Kokuhon Shūsei*: 1997.

Ozaki Ryūen. *Hakuin Zenji Den* (*A Biography of Zen Master Hakuin*). Tokyo: Bummei-dō, 1904.

Rikugawa Taiun. *Hakuin Oshō Shōden* (*Detailed Biography of Zen Master Hakuin*). Tokyo: Sankibō, 1963.

Shōju Rōjin Shū. Tokyo: Shinano kyōiku-kai, 1937.

Takeuchi Naotsugi. *Hakuin.* Tokyo: 1964.

Tōrei Enji. *Hakuin Oshō Nempu* (*Chronological Biography of Zen Priest Hakuin*). Edited by Katō Shōshun. Kyoto: Shibunkaku, 1985.

Yanagida Seizan. *Rinzai no Kafu.* Tokyo: 1970.

Yanagida Seizan and Katō Shōshun. *Hakuin*. Kyoto: 1979.

Yasenkanna furoku (supplement to *Yasenkanna*). Annotated edition of *Idle Talk on a Night Boat* in *Hakuin Zenji Jihitsu Kokuhon Shūsei*: 1996.

Yasenkanna Hyōshaku. Tokyo: Kohaku Dōnin, 1911.

Works in English

Miura, Isshu, and Ruth Sasaki. *Zen Dust*. Kyoto: 1965.

Porkert, Manfred. *The Theoretical Foundations of Chinese Medicine*. Cambridge, Mass.: MIT Press, 1978.

Waddell, Norman. "A Chronological Biography of Zen Priest Hakuin," Parts 1 and 2. (annotated translation of *Hakuin Oshō Nempu*). *Eastern Buddhist* (spring 1994; autumn 1994).

————. *Essential Teachings of Zen Master Hakuin*. Boston: Shambhala Publications, 1994.

————. *Unborn: The Life and Teachings of Zen Master Bankei*. San Francisco: North Point Press, 1980.

————. *Zen Words for the Heart*. Boston: Shambhala Publications, 1996.

Yampolsky, Philip. *Zen Master Hakuin: Selected Writings*. New York: Columbia University Press, 1971.

SEA OF JAPAN

NOTO

ECHIGO

Takada
(Eigan-ji)

Iiyama
(Shōju-an)

ETCHŪ

Takayama

HIDA

KAGA

ECHIZEN

SHINANO

KŌZUKE

MUSASHI

SHIMŌSA

KAZUSA

Edo

SAGAMI

KAI

Mt. Fuji ▲

SURUGA Hara

Shimizu (Shōin-ji)
(Zensō-ji)

IZU

TŌTŌMI

MIKAWA

MINO

Mt. Iwataki
Ōgaki Reishō-in
(Zuiun-ji)

OWARI

SHIMA

Kenkoku-ji

Suzuka Range

IGA

ISE

WAKASA
(Enshō-ji)

Obama

ŌMI

TANGO

TAMBA

Kyoto

KAWACHI

YAMATO

SETTSU

Kaisei-ji

IZUMI

Inryō-ji

Hōun-ji

KII

HARIMA

BITCHŪ

Hōfuku-ji BIZEN

Okayama

SANUKI

AWA

BINGO

BINGO

SHIKOKU

IYO

Matsuyama
(Shōjū-ji)

TOSA

A map of places mentioned in *Wild Ivy*

GLOSSARY AND INDEX

Of People, Places, and Titles Mentioned in the Text

Entries follow, as far as possible, the *furigana* transcriptions found in the 1766 woodblock edition of *Wild Ivy*; entries not appearing in that work follow the readings in Katō Shōshun's *Hakuin Oshō Nempu*.